The Alien Abduction Reference Guide

100 Alien Encounters Explored

Michelle LaVigne-Wedel
Paul Wedel

Sweetgrass Press
P.O. Box 1862
Merrimack, NH 03054

Library of Congress Card Number: 00-192927

Michelle LaVigne-Wedel 1962 -
Paul Wedel 1959 -
The Alien Abduction Reference Guide: 100 Alien Encounters Explored.

ISBN 0-9702630-3-1

1. Unidentified flying objects--Sightings and encounters--Psychological aspects. 2. Abduction--psychological aspects. 3. Victims--Mental health. I. Title

ORIGINAL COVER DESIGN: The Electric Wigwam

Editor: Paul Wedel

Printed in the United States of America

Address all inquiries to:

Sweetgrass Press
P.O. Box 1862
Merrimack, NH 03054
USA

URL: http:// www.sweetgrasspress.com
E-mail: info@sweetgrasspress.com

Paul and Michelle
would like to thank all the wonderful
and courageous people
who contributed and shared events from their
lives.
A special thanks to Dee, Bonnie and "The R Man"
for all your efforts, encouragement and kind words.

ଔ   ଊ

A hello to Teacher, and Profnairb, wherever the
sun greets you today.

Paul and Michelle Wedel
September 2000

Paul Wedel & Michelle LaVigne-Wedel

Both Michelle and Paul are lifelong abduction experiencers who have developed a unique perspective combining common sense, the wisdom of experience and the soul of spirit. Their clear recall and open contact with aliens of several types give them an unequaled mastery of alien contact issues.

Paul Wedel is the author of the ground-breaking book, *Prophecy's Edge*, as well as several websites on UFOlogical and spiritual issues. He authored and designed the highly acclaimed Earthvoices.org —a website where Native American Elders are offered free web pages to post messages that aid the growth of humankind. He has a professional background in computer networking and is an avid canoeist and outdoorsman.

Michelle is the author of such books as the definitive handbook on coping with alien abduction; *The Alien Abduction Survival Guide*. She is also the author of *Lessons* (with Alex) and co-author of *Prophecy's Edge* (with Paul). She has worked in abduction support for almost a decade. She has a professional background as a drafter, technical writer and artist.

When not working, Michelle and Paul spend time with their four children — including their new baby, born in 1999 — camping, canoeing and discovering the wonders of the Mother Earth.

Table of Contents

Foreword

It appears, from the stories that are coming from the alien experiencer community, that the alien abduction phenomenon is soon coming to a climax that will affect everyone. Our little blue planet, as it rides blissfully along the periphery of a small galaxy in a universe too large for any human being's paradigm to comprehend, may well represent the playing field for a much larger agenda.

Surely, with similar accounts of alien contact coming from around the globe, there remains the possibility that such interaction represents much more than mere medical experiments and scientific interest by a foreign culture. When we look at the reports laid out in this book, it becomes clear that we have much more to be concerned with than extraterrestrials poking about our bodies.

The history of the phenomenon demands an answer to the unanswered questions. We do not ask, "Are they here?" For those that have had the experience of alien contact the question is, "I know they are here, but why?" In the face of such a large mystery, the answer lies not with accounts and scientific records of sightings of objects in the sky, but rather with those individuals who have been contacted by the occupants of those alien craft.

Imagine if one day we all were to wake up, turn on our television, and see an international news service broadcasting the landing of aliens on the white house lawn. Everyone would turn to the abductee community in a state of shock and say, "My God, why didn't you tell us it was real?" To which the response will most likely be, "We tried, dear God, we tried."

A reference guide is not only needed, it is a required step in our understanding of the phenomena and how it affects us as a species. With all the fearful accounts of alien abduction that the media has pursued to promote their ratings, they have missed one of the most important steps of all, walking through the fear and facing the truth. Fear sells. Fear draws attention. Fear immobilizes. Fear can rule the majority. However, the majority rule does not make truth.

The Alien Abduction Reference Guide seeks to draw us one step closer to the truth about alien abductions. It seeks to walk through the fear and print the accounts of contactee's who remember the extraterrestrial bases they were on, their interactions with the aliens and humans in that environment, as well as the training and spiritual evolution they have gone through during their experiences. This is a book that all people interested in UFOlogy can reference, as it draws from the experiences of people from around the world. This book is a reference guide for the new millennium.

Paul Wedel
September 1999

Introduction

You turn on your television to find yet another show about alien abduction. You watch the screen, transfixed, as the word "reenactment" pops up at the bottom of the screen and a strange blue light shines through the bedroom window of the unsuspecting television show victim. A person on the bed lays motionless and unable to move, while a group of small, thin, gray skinned beings enter their room and surround the bed. The camera cuts to a view of the poor victim's face. The fear in her eyes makes it clear that she wants to scream but cannot utter a sound. The scene changes and our helpless victim is now on a craft with these little beings running around her. The scene cuts once again. Now we see a person sitting in a dark room. Her face is scrambled. She says, "They took eggs from my ovaries!"

You think to yourself, "Geeze, same old thing," and you change the channel.

Did you ever wonder if the story really ends there? Have you ever wondered what else happens to these people when they are in the company of their ET captors? Have you ever pondered if the people on these shows know more than they are telling? The truth is, there is more to the story of alien contact; there is much more.

If we look back to the past, we see that the abduction phenomena has changed over and over again through the years. In the 1940's and 1950's, the people who claimed to have contact often talked about human-like aliens who were visiting Earth from nearby worlds. They talked of peace and intergalactic brotherhood. By and large, the opinion of the

i

general public at the time was that these people were just making it up or simply 'kooks'.

In the 1960's and 1970's, with the appearance of such encounters as Betty and Barney Hill's abduction, suddenly peoples' attention focused on diminutive, gray ETs with big black eyes who collect humans for medical experiments. The horror of this newly reported type of experience, and the sense of *science* it seemed to hold with its medical theme and doctor-like aliens, was somehow more easily accepted by the general public. It seemed more plausible that if aliens were coming to earth, they were coming to study us, rather than befriend us.

Although the Hill event pushed alien abduction into the faces of the general public, and though it was more accepted than the *galactic brotherhood aliens* of the 1950's, it was still far from being accepted as truth. Anyone who dared to say they had alien contact was once again labeled unkindly.

In the 1980's, much of the focus around the abduction phenomena still revolved around the fact that gray ETs were doing medical work on their human 'guinea pigs'. With the advent of television shows on the subject, and many books about abductions, more and more people began to come quietly forward with their experiences. But by and large, if any experience they recalled did not wholly fit the standard template of what researchers believed happened during abductions, their accounts were swept aside as fantasy or prevarication.

Although theories abounded and were wide-ranging as to who the aliens were and where they come from, overall, those who believed in ETs, believed they were here for one thing — medical research. To be a contactee who deviated from that one thing was a quick way to discredit yourself in the eyes of all.

The 1990's ushered in a new era of Ufology. With the emergence of such men as Dr. John E. Mack M.D. into the arena of abduction study, suddenly the focus reached beyond 'who are these alien visitors.' Now researchers began to ask more important questions such as, "How does the contact experience affect those humans involved?" and "What can be done to help these people?" and arguably, even more importantly, "What else is involved in the abduction event beyond medical experiments, and why?"

By the end of the 1990's the focus, for many, was no longer making people believe that UFO's were real, but rather, helping those having contact and learning from these individuals what they gleaned from their experiences.

By the turn of the century, the new attitude of exploration of the experience emerged as a driving force. In the new millennium, rather than pigeon holing those whose memories extend beyond the limits of the medical abduction template as *kooks*, *crazies* or *wannabees*, researchers are starting to listen to these individuals. What they are finding is amazing.

Unfortunately, for the most part, these aspects of the abduction experience are totally disregarded and ignored by the mainstream media, who continue to report about the medical aspects of encounters as if they are the only thing that happen. It is no secret to any abductee who has worked with the media that many hours of valuable information about the contact experience lays wasted on the cutting room floor.

Likewise, many pages of experiences submitted to researchers from abductees about their non-medical accounts lay collecting dust in drawers or have been dismissed as bogus and tossed out long ago.

Things such as ET classrooms, ET built amusement parks and even whole cities are common settings remembered by abductees. Yet, these type of accounts have typically been dismissed by mainstream UFOlogist as nothing more than dreams or delusions. Such accounts are proving to be more.

As more and more abductees come forward with their detailed recall of alien contact that is not solely of a medical nature, the picture of who these aliens could be, what they want, and why they are here begins to unfold.

In the following pages, you will find one hundred such detailed events. We did our best to group them into categories, but some crossover. Every event you will read is an actual, real event from someone's life. The subjects of these events range in age from seven years old to more than seventy, and are from both sexes, several sexual preferences, and a wide range of religious (or non-religious) and income groups. Several countries are represented., but by and large, the majority of the subjects come from the United States, Canada and Great Britain. We did not add or alter the content of their accounts in any way beyond basic editing for publication.

Each subject was promised total confidentiality. That is why no names are used in the events. All identifying information has been removed. (With the exception of events from our own lives). Paul and I believe that total confidentiality is important as many of the subjects in this book do not wish to make their contactee status known. Our promise of total confidentiality also assured that the subjects did not have a motive to withhold details of their experiences.

If the event was personal to Paul or Michelle, our names are used and the event is told from the first person point of view.

You may be surprised by how detailed the accounts in this book are. This is because, with few exceptions, they are all events that were consciously recalled by the subject at the time of the event, or remembered subsequently without the aid of hypnotic regression.

By the time you are done reading this book you will know there is far more to the abduction experience than medical experiments; maybe a lot more than you ever imagined; certainly a great deal more than you are likely to see on television.

Chapter 1
Experiments

When beginning a collection of abduction events, it is fitting to start with the more familiar — experiments. By and large, the topic of alien experiments on humans has been the focus of much of the literature available on the contact phenomena. When examining the list of experiments that abductees undergo, it is easy to be led into believing that medical procedures — such as the extraction of genetic material — are the only things that people endure. This is, in part, because it is what the media chooses to talk about, so it is what many will remember first. It is also, in part, because people who do remember more are not motivated to talk about it, as they will often be told that they are dreaming or making it up because their experiences do not fall into the expected set of encounters.

Though the extraction of genetic material is a very common procedure, there are many other medical procedures contactees are subject to, such as the flushing of the digestive system and the implantation of alien devices into the body. The reasons for some of these may seem obvious, others may be harder to fathom.

We offer you the idea that not all experiments are medical or for a medical purpose, though some clearly are. The question of medical encounters should be; why are they doing what they do? Is there any benefit to the human subjects?

Through this book, you will find encounters in other sections that have an underlying experimental nature, but they were put in other areas because the focus of the event seemed to be something other than the medical procedure — at least for the abductee.

The question of an *alien agenda* must be explored when looking at any stories of ET experimentation on the human race. We must ask ourselves things like:

◆What benefit do the aliens glean from these experiments?

◆How many times do they have to perform the same test and on how many humans do they have to perform it before they come to a conclusion?

◆Do the aliens know about statistics? If so, why are they not able to find their results after so many tests, based on population and statistical numbers?

◆Could it be something totally alien to human thinking? Could it be that those things they do, that we as humans perceive of as experiments, are actually something totally different?

Keep an open mind and try not to think in the box that is human understanding, being ever mindful that aliens may, by their very nature, not think the same way as humans. Thus, things that seem obvious to humans, may not even occur to the alien mind.

Section 1.1 Medical Tests

In section 1 of this chapter, we offer you examples of encounters that represent a cross section of some of the lesser known medical procedures that abductees endure. Although there are only one of each kind, we have received reports of many similar events.

Event 1
Subject: Michelle
Date: 1993
Location: United States

(Comment: This is an example of an implantation of an alien device. It implies that aliens know and are mindful of which contactees are subjects of human research and which are not.

Is their concern merely that they will be found out? Though one might assume so, some contactees have been told that they are kept in the dark about such things for their own protection. Otherwise, their quiet lives would be inundated with everyone from the curious to the unstable.

The next question becomes, what are these devices for? If we can assume they monitor human activity and condition, then we have to ask, why do they care about an individual's condition?)

I was woken up by a small gray alien gently pulling my hair to get my attention. I stood up to go with him then found myself on shipboard. I was sitting in a waiting room area. There were several people there, but no one was talking to me. I sat for a while until it was my turn to go into the examination room. When it was my turn, I was asked to sit in a big chair. It was really soft, as if it were a vinyl bag full of jelly. I sank into the chair. My right foot was lifted onto an extension that was attached to the chair.

I asked the gray being who moved my foot, "What are you going to do to me?"

He said, "We are going to put something into your ankle. But you won't remember it and won't know it is there."

"Will it hurt when you put it in? Will I feel it later?" I asked with concern.

"No," he said quickly, "there will be no effects."

I wanted to watch and see how they did it, so I leaned over as best as I could. The little gray being was holding a small white instrument in his hand that was flattened out at an angle on one end and rounded on the other. It was only about five inches long.

He held the instrument, flat end first, toward my inner right ankle. I watched as he used the end of the instrument to cut into my ankle, peal back the skin, and expose the bone. I felt nothing. He touched the bone with the flat end of the instrument and a piece of bone chipped off and fell to the floor. There was no blood and no pain, even though it looked very painful.

Hetar, the tall gray alien I work with, came into the room and check on what was happening. I was not the only person in the room and he stopped and looked at several other people before he came over to me. By the time he got to me, the little gray had taken a small flat object and pushed it into the exposed, soft part of the bone in my ankle, then turned the instrument so it was facing, round end, toward me. He began waving it over the bone. The bone seemed to be growing over the device he just put into my ankle.

Hetar came over and started to talk to the little gray. He told the smaller being to be especially careful not to leave any scars or marks on me because I was the subject of some research and he didn't want to leave any unnecessary clues. The little one nodded. They talked some more, but I didn't understand much of what they were saying. As they talked, the little one seemed to loose track of what he was doing and he grew too much bone on my ankle. As a result, there was an odd lump on the ankle. Hetar motioned to him and he turned the instrument away from my ankle and flipped it over in his hand in one quick motion.

Both he and Hetar touched my anklebone. Hetar didn't seem to think it was too much of a problem I guess, because he said something else to the smaller gray and then walked away.

The smaller gray appeared to try and even off the lump, then put the skin of my ankle back into position. He turned the instrument — round side forward — and used it to make the skin mend shut. There was no mark left behind, but there was an odd lump on my anklebone that stuck out quite a bit.

For weeks after this event the odd lump on my ankle bothered me because it rubbed on my high-topped sneakers. Once in a while, if I banged my ankle, I felt an abnormally sharp pain shoot up my leg. Several weeks after the implant was put in, I was picked up again and the bone growth was re-shaped to a more normal size.

Event 2
Subject: Paul
Date: 1996
Location: Canada

(Comment: We have received many reports of people either having needles put into their eyes, or watching others have this procedure done. Though Paul was told they were putting a camera in his eye, some abductees are told that

they are fixing everything from blood pressure problems to adjusting vision.

Based on these reports, it would seem that the aliens have a level of concern for contactees, to the extent of intervention to improve their health.)

I found myself in a room with several gray ET's and a human woman who I knew very well. She was staring at me intensely. I was staring back and focusing my attention on the pair of eyes in front of me. Her gaze was calming me and helping me stay controlled for something that was about to occur.

After a couple of minutes, I lay down flat on a table. There were several grays attending to me. I tried to remain calm as they lowered a mask over my face. At first, my teeth started to chatter. My attention began to break down and fear got a hold of me. The plate-like mask was put over my face. I knew it was a device the ETs used to steady a long needle that was inserted into the eyeball. They told me they were going to use it to embed a small camera like device into my eye so they could see out of my eyes whenever it was necessary.

The thought of having a long needle inserted into my eye was terrifying. My focus soon broke down completely and I panicked. I even started to cry.

The woman climbed up on top of me and straddled across my chest. She continued to stare deeply into my eyes. I heard one of the aliens say in an annoyed tone, "The tears are going to ruin the procedure."

"Be still!" the woman commanded the alien.

"Look at me!" she said to me sternly.

I stared back at her and began to calm down. She helped me regain my focus and soon I was okay. The mask was put completely over my face and I was able to lie there patiently. Some time passed where I felt no pain whatsoever. Soon the mask was removed and one of the aliens standing next to the woman said, "It's all done."

I was greatly relieved and emotionally worn.

Event 3
Subject: Adult Female
Date: 1998
Location: United Kingdom

(Comment: Many contactees report being covered or submerged in a thick liquid. This event is unusual in the fact that the subject helped coat herself. Notice that when the subject refused to allow her face to be covered, her consciousness fades. This is an example of what we have come to call "stress amnesia".

It is common for some abductees to loose consciousness when they are made to experience things they do not want to do. The question to ask is, do the ETs or the subject create this? You may be quick to answer it is the aliens doing, but if that were so, why wouldn't all abductees have stress amnesia?

With this in mind, consider that the aliens may not be totally lying when the say that the decision as to whether an event is remembered or not is not always their choice.)

The subject found herself feeling hot and tingly. She realized she was feeling paralyzed and felt her body floating. The next thing she recalled was sitting on a white table. A tall gray alien being was there, as were two or three small grays. The tall being walked away, leaving the little ones in charge.

The smaller aliens started to put a white, slimy liquid over her body. She was curious to know what the liquid was, but she was feeling rather sleepy and did not have the energy to ask. After a few moments, she started feeling better and sat up to watch the aliens as they rubbed the liquid onto her legs.

They had started to apply the liquid at her feet and were working their way upward. She joined in and helped them rub the liquid onto her legs. She was concerned because she noticed that they had missed a few spots. They didn't seem to mind her helping out and made no effort to stop her.

They continued to put the liquid on until her whole body was covered, with the exception of her face. The subject told them she didn't want any of the liquid to be put on her face because she was afraid it would give her pimples. She reported the liquid seemed to feel very greasy. The little gray aliens seemed to be at a loss for what to do when she refused.

The taller gray being came back and told her to go to sleep. Her memory became cloudy at that point. She vaguely recalled walking outside her house and hugging the taller gray alien before lying down in her own bed for the remainder of the night.

Event 4
Subject: Adult Female
Date: 1993
Location: United States

(Comment: Consider the impurities mentioned below. What could the aliens be doing that they would consider such things impurities? Do certain hormones interfere with their work? We have received several reports of women who were not lactating being asked to nurse alien, half-breed

babies. We also received reports from woman who began lactating without pregnancy. Could the "impurities" removed from this woman be used to create lactation in other women?

What purpose does it serve the aliens to have woman hold, feed and give attention to infants in their environment? Could the benefits be intended for the infants?)

A twenty-six year old woman was abducted and in the company of gray aliens. She was asked to sit on a large, soft chair that appeared to be made of some kind of gel-like plastic. Her body sunk into the chair and she was unable to move. A taller ET, who she identified as the head doctor, came over to her and put some kind of device on her upper arm. She described it as looking much like a bandage. It was connected to a very thin tube that ran into some machine.

"What are you doing?" she asked the gray.

"We are removing the impurities from your blood so you can do your work," the gray replied.

She assumed he was talking about germs or viruses and was relieved that if she did have any impurities in her blood, they were being removed.

After the procedure was done, the woman was led to another room by a smaller gray alien. As she walked into the next room, her memory went blank. It returned as she was being led back into the room with the big, soft chair.

She was once again placed into the chair so that she could not move. The bandage like device was put back on her upper arm and the machine was once again put on.

She said she turned to the tall gray and asked, "Are you removing more impurities from my blood?"

"No," the gray replied, "it is returning your impurities to your body."

"But what if I don't want them back? I don't want impurities in my blood!" she insisted.

"The impurities we removed are necessary for lactation. Without these impurities you would not be able to produce milk for your child," the gray explained.

The woman said she sat still for the remainder of the experience. Later, she was led to a room with curving white walls and was instructed to sit on a bench that was molded from the wall.

She did not recall how she was returned home.

Section 1.2   Reaction Tests

In section 2 of this chapter, we offer you examples of encounters that represent a cross section of some of the strange events abductees endure that seem to be designed to train them or measure their reaction to something. Often, these events revolve around saving themselves or others. These tests cross over into visions of the end of the world. (Editors note: Experiences that are particular to *apocalyptic visions* are in chapter 4.)

After reading many events of these types of tests, we have come to the conclusion that they are some kind of controlled environment created to test and teach people skills they will need in some future time.

It appears that the aliens do not want to leave much to chance and need to know that people will react a certain way under certain circumstances. In order to assure this, they place these people into the illusion of such events and watch how things unfold.

People are subjected to the same test events over and over again. Sometimes they have slight differences. But by and large, they are the same event, or at least the same theme. Most experiencers report that these events started, or became more noticeable, in their teenage years and are ongoing. Ongoing of events are not given dates.

Many contactees have repetitious events and tests. They may think of them as reoccurring dreams. Though many abductees reported dreams that we suspect are actually memories of reaction tests, we have only included stories from people who know, beyond a shadow of a doubt, they were with the aliens when the event started, or after it was over.

Event 5
Subject: Adult Female
Date: Reoccurring
Location: United States
(Comment: Many people reported events like the two that follow. The story is always the same. They are in charge of saving a group of people from some kind of terrible disaster — natural or man made. The events always involve intense fear, along with an overwhelming need to save the people.

Are these tests to see if a person has the ability to save others or training exercises? Either way, it would seem the aliens want to make sure there are individuals who are able to take charge and save other humans in time of turmoil.)

During an alien contact, the subject reported that she found herself standing in a building. It seemed like a big building that was built downward into the ground. There were hundreds of people around her. There was some kind of horrible catastrophe happening outside the building, and the only way to save the people was to make them go down into the depths of the building. But the people didn't want to go, because they were afraid.

The subject felt she had to save all the people. She pushed some into elevators and forced others to go down the stairs. They resisted her, but she kept pushing them to go. All the while, she was shouting to them that it was the only way to save their lives.

The subject knew, beyond a doubt, that if she didn't get the people underground soon, they were going to die. She also knew that she could not get to shelter herself until all the people were safe. Yet, she knew if she stayed above ground too much longer, she herself would die.

She had to fight with them, and push them. After she got the people to safety, she woke up to find herself with the aliens. Each time this reaction test ended, they would tell her if she did good or not so good.

Event 6
Subject: Paul
Date: 1997
Location: Canada

(Comment: As you can see, the theme of this event is much like the previous one. In this event, two individuals join together and work as a team to save the people.)

I knew aliens had abducted me. I saw them in my room, then I blacked out. I awoke to find myself in a tan colored room that had many different panels and doorway hatches. All of them were closed. There were approximately fifteen other men and women in the room with me.

Suddenly, all the hatches started opening and closing by themselves. A moment later, I heard a woman scream. Terror filled the room. We all looked around frantically for an exit. A door opened behind me to my left. The people around me were paralyzed with fear. It seemed like the only reason for their fear was that the hatches were opening and closing on their own.

Another man and I took control of ourselves and began to file people out of the open door behind me. It took every ounce of strength to battle my paralyzing terror.

Some of the people who I helped were so scared they could barely move their arms and legs. The other man and I grabbed them and dragged them through the door. At some points we were literally throwing people through the door.

Finally, when the last person was out, I had a one sentence argument with the other man about which one of us should exit first. Before it was settled, the man pushed me through the door.

Once we were both on the other side, the man and I started to herd the people away from the door. I looked back and saw that the door was in the hull of some type of craft. The overwhelming terror I was experiencing made it so difficult that it took all my emotional strength to look back through the door.

Event 7
Subject: Adult Female
Date: 1996
Location: United States

(Comment: The following is an example of another common reaction test. This subject was told to do something she didn't want to do. When she refused, she was told her life depended on it. In an odd twist, the subject did not believe it. More often than not, the contactee believes it and does what is asked.

The benefit to the subject is harder to see here. Since the subject did not complete the task at hand, we have no way of knowing the total point of the experience.)

The subject reported she was taken by aliens to a downtown shopping area of a city that looked human made. She described the city as looking like it came straight out of the 1950's.

She reported that she was told to enter a particular building by the aliens. She found the building and entered it. Inside, there was an old escalator that led to the second floor. The escalator was made of wood and didn't seem very sturdy to the subject, nevertheless, she rode the escalator to the second floor.

At the top, there was what the subject described as a cargo net. She needed to climb it to get to the next floor. There was nothing between the cargo net and the bottom floor. There was no actual second floor. She reported seeing several people climbing on the net. They seemed to be having fun, or at least oblivious to the danger they were in.

The subject said she didn't want to climb the net, so she turned around and rushed back down the escalator.

When she got to the bottom, she was greeted by a gray alien. He quietly, and without emotion, said to her, "You have been poisoned. The cure for your poison is on the third floor on the other side of that net." He then caused her to visualize a green bottle of liquid. The gray explained that if she made it across the net to the green bottle she would live. It was her only hope.

The subject reported that she believed he was lying. She believed he was just telling her she was poisoned to make her go over the net. She felt he was doing that because he could sense she was afraid to go and wanted to give her some incentive to face that fear.

She refused to go.

The gray then said, "You are going to die in six minutes if you don't go."

The subject said she stood there and started to count off the seconds of the six minutes. She reported the gray became perturbed. It was as if he didn't know how to deal with her and was becoming frustrated.

She continued to count. When she got close to four minutes she said to the gray, "I don't feel sick at all."

The gray said, "It will hit you like a switch at exactly six minutes. You should go before it is too late."

She still refused to go. Just before she reached six minutes she reported becoming very dizzy. The gray then said to her, "Are you going to climb the net yet?"

She replied, "I can't. It's too late. I'm dying." She blacked out and woke in her bed. She went to her bathroom and checked herself in the mirror to see if she was physically okay. She returned to her bed, fell asleep and dreamed she was climbing the cargo net.

The subject reported that the next time she was contacted, she was once again brought to the same city setting. There she saw several women riding horses. When they saw her, they dismounted their horses and asked her if she wanted to join them inside the same building. The subject refused, saying she didn't want to have to deal with the cargo net again. Her memory then ends.

Event 8
Subject: Adult Female
Date: 1966
Location: United States

(Comment: The following reaction test could easily be placed in section 4.2 Apocalyptic Visions. It is here because the focus of the event is not so much the apocalyptic but rather moral choices.

When reading the following, question what benefit creating such an event would have for the aliens? What does this woman's choice say about her courage and her compassion? Lastly, what would you have done in such a situation?

It is clear the subject was upset by this test, as most anyone would be. Nevertheless, the subject said that she realized after this test that the lives she saved were important, too. She also said that since she did not know where her own children were, she did not regret her choice.)

The subject reported that she was in the company of the gray aliens. They told her to look at a screen, much like a movie screen. She did. Suddenly she forgot she was with the aliens and believed she was standing in an unfamiliar city. Air raid sirens started to blare. The subject was washed with panic and began to run around the town looking for the school where her children were. She did not know where the school was.

She was in a blind panic. She knew there was only a short time before everyone who had not found shelter would be killed. She found a school and saw two children there who were not her own, but who needed help. She realized that no parent came to get them. The subject reported that she was greatly torn between helping these children and finding her own. She knew she could not just leave them, but knew that if she didn't hurry, she would never find and save her own children.

She looked at the children again and prayed someone would give compassion to her children and save them the way she was about to save these children. The subject then grabbed the two children and ran for the shelter of a basement in the school building.

As she ran, the vision of her own two children standing in a school yard, confused, alone and afraid filled her mind. The subject was washed with pain and anxiety. She told the two children she brought to the basement to stay there until she returned.

The subject then ran out from the shelter of the basement to continue the search for her own children. She ran through the empty playground, but before she got more than a few strides, she saw a bright flash, then a roaring heat washed over her. She knew she was dead.

She opened her eyes and found she was sitting with the aliens. One of the taller aliens looked at her and said, "Your heart is good. This is good."

The subject reported that she spat at him.

Event 9
Subject: Adult Female
Date: 1996
Location: United States

(Comment: Was this a test of loyalty? Was it a test of vanity? Was it truly a person saving the world? Several people have reported events where they were asked to do something to save the world that would surely cause their own deaths, only to be 'saved' by the aliens at the last minute.

Is selflessness an important part of whatever it is the aliens are training humans for with these reaction tests?)

The subject reported she found herself standing in a big, open area, inside a building of some kind. There was a door behind her. It was heavy and metal, like a bank vault. She looked around, but other than the closed metal door, and a glass door that led out to a parking lot area, there was nothing in the building.

She walked outside to find the parking lot empty except for a small guard shack next to a tall fence that ringed the building. She walked to the shack and was surprised to find that inside sat the taller gray alien she described as "her alien."

The subject asked the being what was going on. He told her that she was there to do a job. She had to go back into the building and open the large metal door. Behind it she would find a jar-like object. She was to put the lid back onto the object, secure it tightly, then bring it out to him. He warned her that the jar was dangerous and she would be poisoned by it. He also told her that if she did not go and get the jar, its poison would spread across the face of the Earth and kill everyone.

She reported she felt a strong sense that what he was saying about the world was true and she had to do something to save it. She agreed to do it.

The subject reported she went back into the building and opened the metal door. It was at least two feet thick, but moved very easily when she pulled at it. Behind the door she reported finding a small table with what looked like a brown mason jar sitting on it. The cover for the jar lay on the floor, next to the table. She picked up the cover and placed it onto the jar. Then she used a wire-like device that was attached to the jar to secure the lid, in much the same way one would close a mason jar.

She then reported bringing the jar back to the gray alien. He told her to put it down on the ground outside the shack and come in and sit down because he had something to tell her.

She entered the shack and sat on a stool. The gray then told her that the jar contained a very deadly form of radioactive material and she would die in less than twelve minutes.

She was in shock. She knew he said it was deadly, but she felt she would have time to say goodbye to her friends and family. She said to the alien, "I thought I would have time to say goodbye and let the world know what I did."

The gray asked, "Would you have saved the world if you knew you would not get credit for it?"

She didn't know what to say, so she didn't answer. After a few moments of silence the gray asked her, "Are you going to cry and beg for a cure?"

She reported answering, "No. What is the point. I'm dead now. I was dead when I opened that door!"

The gray then said to her, "I forgot. I have a cure for you." He handed her a white pill that looked like an aspirin caplet. "This will cure you and you will have no ill effects from your exposure to the jar or its contents," he explained as he handed her the pill.

The subject swallowed the pill then became dizzy. The next place she was aware of being, was on her sofa at home.

Event 10
Subject: Adult Male
Date: 1989
Location: Australia

(Comment: In the following event, the subject is given a reaction test that causes him to appreciate what he has before he looses it.

Consider who benefited from this. What did the aliens gain by bringing this boy together with his grandfather? If it was not for their benefit, could they have done it out of compassion for the old man, and his grandson?)

The subject, who is an Australian aboriginal, reported that when he was a teen, his grandfather used to want to talk to him about his people and their traditional ways, but he never wanted to listen. He said he didn't have time to sit all day and listen to the ramblings of an old man. Besides, he wanted to be more modern and didn't care much about it. Because of this, he avoided his grandfather, and ignored the old man much of the time.

During an abduction event, the gray aliens took him into a room and showed him the dead body of this grandfather. The aliens said nothing. The subject felt not only sad at loosing his grandfather, but also realized that he had not learned anything from his grandfather, and now that knowledge was gone. The subject reported that he was suddenly overcome with a feeling of great loss for what he would never know.

The aliens brought him home and he fell asleep. When he woke the next morning, he was afraid to go next door to his grandfather's home, in fear of finding the old man dead, like he saw the night before. But he knew he had to.

To his surprise and delight, his grandfather was not dead. From that point on, the subject spent as much time as he could with his grandfather, learning things he now valued.

Event 11
Subject: Adult Male
Date: 1995
Location: United States

(Comment: The purpose of this man's reaction test is obvious. The aliens valued him enough to save his life.

It should be noted that incidents like this indicate that the aliens appear to know future events. This is an important fact to extract from reaction tests. If this man's event was practice for something that was really going to happen — which it proved to be — then what about those of others?)

The subject reported that he was with the gray aliens. They told him to sit down in a large chair and then he fell into a vision. He believed he was standing in his own driveway. He was home from work early. There was a car parked in front of his house, but he didn't think much of it, since he lived on a crowed street and many times neighbors and their guests parked in front of his house.

When he walked into the house, he was shocked to find his wife with another man. He ran to the man and started to beat him. A fight started and the man pulled out a gun from his clothing. The subject struggled with the man for the gun, but could not get it away. The gun fired and the subject was fatally hit. He awoke from the vision to find himself in the company of the aliens.

He demanded to know what was going on and why they showed him that. They did not answer.

He was abducted several more times, only to be subjected to the same event. Each time he struggled with the man and was shot to death.

The subject reported that less than one year after this string of events with the aliens, he came home from work early when his company had a power failure. When he arrived home, there was a car outside his house and he remembered the events the aliens made him experience.

He walked into the house, all the while bracing himself. He expected to find his wife with another man. He was not wrong. He did find her with another man.

Remembering the events from the alien encounters, he did not struggle with the man, but rather shouted at his wife and left the house.

Though his marriage was not repairable, he managed to keep his life. The subject was sure that if he would have followed his instincts and fought with the man, he would have been killed

Section 1.3 Sexual Tests

In section 3 of this chapter, we offer you seven very different examples of encounters that represent a cross section of many of the sexually based events contactees are subject to.

On the surface, it is easy to accuse the aliens of not having any regard for our human sexuality. But as we read more and more events, we came to see that the aliens seem to be perplexed by the vast diversity of human sexual behavior.

Of all the things in mankind's (and womankind's) existence, sexual behavior and sexual morals are the most divergent of all beliefs. From person to person in the same cultural background and environment, what is considered sexually acceptable will vary greatly.

Often, sex and love are thought of as the same thing. For some people you cannot have one without the other. Even so, many people draw differences between sexual wants and love desires.

For example, some people who would never dream of cheating on their spouse or significant other may fantasize about encounters with a co-worker or movie star. Other people, who profess to love their spouses deeply, have sexual affairs behind their spouse's back without guilt over their disloyalty. These inconsistencies appear to confuse the alien visitors, who seem to make sexually moral gaffe after gaffe, never catching on to what is acceptable and why.

Then again, could this confusion on their part only be some kind of guise in order to explore the lengths of human sexual behavior on an individual basis?

Could it be that the aliens are trying to understand the concepts of love held by each individual. Could these events be some kind of testing of a person's limits and understanding of love? Could they be assessing each individual's perspective of sexual behavior and how it relates to love?

Could it be that the grays understand our sexual preference as a people, but don't understand that there are varying views in individuals?

Could it simply be that they are trying to push us to ask difficult questions of ourselves and our own understanding of lovemaking versus physical pleasure.

Could it be something totally different?

If we are to believe not only what the aliens tell us , but also many human philosophers and religious heads over the ages, we are all beings of energy in corporeal form. We are souls of light in bodies of flesh. The way we choose to offer, expend and otherwise share that energy with others could, if we choose, take on a sexual form.

The aliens may find it perplexing that most abductees are not reluctant to share the important part of themselves - their souls - with others, but are particular as to who they allow access to their physical container.

Some abductees reported that they found themselves in intimate situations with other abductees on shipboard, where they wanted to intermix with the other persons "energy" much more than they wanted the sexual encounter, but the sexual encounter was the only way they could obtain that intermixing effectively.

When we add the factor of soul energy interactions into the following events, they become not only more complex, but also more understandable from a human perspective.

The accounts that follow are of a sexual nature, but are not sexually explicit. We tried to be considerate of those who are embarrassed by such things or are under age. Nevertheless, please be advised that they do have sexual content.

Event 12
Subject: Adult Female
Date: 1999
Location: United Kingdom

(Comment: This next event illustrates a common event people report. They are asked to have sex in front of a group that watches. Many do without arguing — as this subject did — regardless of the fact that most would never do such a thing in their Earth life.

We also have received several reports from people who were asked to watch other humans having sexual intercourse. Could some of those people be among the group mentioned below?

If energy interaction is the focus, then could the woman in this event be a student, showing her teachers what she has learned? Perhaps she is a teacher, demonstrating a technique to her audience.

When you consider the number of people who report these types of events, it is not very likely that the subject is merely involved in an experiment to see how humans have sex, nor is it likely she is entertainment for the aliens watching.)

The subject woke up at about 3 a.m. in the morning. She reported that she saw a bright light coming from outside. Soon, she felt herself being pulled upward through her window. The next thing she recalled was waking up on a examination table. She reported seeing two small grays walking away from her as she came to.

She said she sensed many beings had entered the room. She looked toward them and noticed that they were all of varying heights and types. Some were human looking, some looked like hybrids, and some were the tall grays.

They asked her questions, but the subject did not remember what the questions were. Then they led her boyfriend into the room. She was surprised to see him.

Her boyfriend joined her on the table. They were somehow made to feel like having sex. So they did. The beings stood round them and watched.

The next morning the subject reported that when she saw her boyfriend he told her that he had a dream that they had sex while many people watched.

Event 13
Subject: Adult Male
Date: 1996
Location: United Kingdom

(Comment: The following two events are examples of times when it appears the aliens used sex as a distraction while some other procedure was done. Sexual encounters being used as a distraction — particularly in men — is rather common.

The next two examples came from men who live in different countries and have not had contact with each other at the time of their report. The similarities are striking. Both men recalled the events with the focus on the sexual aspect, rather than any medical procedure that could be happening.

In both examples telepathy was involved. In the first example, the subject did not have actual dialogue with either the aliens or his sexual partner, but circumstantial evidence was left behind.)

The subject had been experiencing feelings of anxiety all night. The subject described these feelings as *the creeps.* Earlier that night he saw a strange light in the sky, moving in a strange matter. The subject said when he saw strange lights in the sky, he would have contact soon after. It was as if the lights heralded the event.

After some time, he went to bed and fell asleep. He started having a strange feeling, as if he were being stared at, but he could not open his eyes. The next thing he reported was having a very erotic feeling, as if someone was touching him in a sexual way. The feeling was very physical — more so than an average sexual dream — yet he still could not open his eyes.

He repeated to himself, "I've got to open my eyes."

There was a voice in his head that said, "Don't open your eyes. If you are enjoying this dream, why wake up?"

Later, he heard a voice say, "You can open your eyes now."

When he did, he found there was an alien female on top of him. He reported she was extremely thin, with a large head and tufts of red hair. He described her as looking like a mix of a gray and a human, but more gray then human. She was totally naked, but had little in the way of female attributes, such as breasts.

The subject reported the female's most noticeable feature was her eyes. He said they were strikingly beautiful. They were large, round and looked human in every way, except for their size. He explained they gave her an appearance similar to that of a Japanese cartoon illustration.

He said her most disturbing feature was her misshapen mouth, with odd shaped teeth that were widely spaced, crooked and crossing in places.

The subject said that he was experiencing very different, unresolved emotions at the time. Part of him was enthralled by her eyes and the physical sensation. Another part of him was about as terrified as he had ever been in his life.

As this was happening, the subject realized someone, or something, was holding his head at both sides near his ears. He could not move his head on his own.

Whatever was holding him began to tilt his head from one side to the other. The subject noted that something was being done to his head. He was so enthralled with the woman he could not focus enough attention on his head to figure out what was going on.

When the work on his head stopped and he could once again move, the subject reported that the alien woman astride him nodded. When she did, he experienced an intense orgasm, then blacked out and didn't wake until morning.

When he woke the next morning, his underwear was on the ground. He knew beyond a doubt that he was wearing them when he went to bed the previous night.

Event 14
Subject: Adult Male
Date: 1996
Location: Canada

(Comment: Just as in the last event, sex is used to distract the subject from a physical procedure being done. In this second example, the subject had actual dialogue with the aliens and his sexual partner.)

The encounter took place in the subject's house. In the middle of the night he opened his eyes to find his house completely lit up. His consciousness seemed very dream-like, almost like he was doped up. Nevertheless, he could see everything clearly and was unquestionably awake.

He reported that he watched as a number of small gray aliens set up a table in his hallway. He got up and walked to the hall. Once there, the aliens explained something to him that he found of great interest at the time, but soon forgot after the experience ended.

He reported that communication was transmitted telepathically. No verbal words were spoken. In the middle of the conversation with the grays in the hallway, a very tall woman with dark hair walked into his room and stood beside him. She was well over six feet tall. Her head came close to the ceiling. He reported that she was very beautiful.

"Who is this?" the man asked a gray who was standing nearby.

"She will be with you," he responded. The thought behind his response was clearly that of a sexual nature.

"I don't understand. What? I mean why?" he replied to the gray, then turned to the woman. "Wouldn't it be better if you liked me?" he asked her. He was completely bewildered as to why she wanted to be with him.

She put her hand on his shoulder and said, "But I do like you."

He began to get more confused. It was clear she was hearing his thoughts. He stopped short and thought to her, "Okay, fine. I'm not going to ask any questions. I'll believe it when I see it."

The subject reported that everything went black. The next thing he recalled was opening his eyes and seeing the woman's face right in front of him. She had a huge smile on her face. Her mouth looked strange. It was as if she had several dozen, oddly spaced teeth. Her eyes were peculiar, in that her pupils seemed to be somewhat oval. He realized she wasn't fully human.

She leaned her body down over top of him and proceeded to become physically amorous with him. The subject reported the sensation was extremely physical. After a period of time she lay back on the bed and pulled him closer to her. He tried to respond, but was having trouble physically functioning.

"Make love to me," he heard her say with a thought. He changed somehow when she said this and became physically functional, as well as emotionally wanting.

It was then he realized that someone was standing near his head. They were inserting a long object — like a needle — into his jawbone from an area behind his ear.

The subject then blacked out and awoke to find everyone was gone and the event was over. There was no evidence that anything occurred.

Event 15
Subject: Adult Male
Date: 1996
Location: United States

(Comment: Could this example of an alien sexual faux-pas actually be an attempt at compassion? The subject was left with that impression. Most who have this type of experience are left with the same impression, whether or not they were angered by the intrusion.)

The subject reported that he was away on business, and staying in a hotel. He was lying in bed, thinking about his wife and how much he missed her. He believed he drifted into thought, but he knew he had not fallen asleep. He heard something and looked to see his wife standing by the door. He didn't think to wonder why or how she was there. It was as if that part of his reasoning was turned off.

Instead, he was so glad to see her that he grabbed her, hugged her, then made love to her.

During the sexual act, he realized that something didn't feel right. Even though the person looked like his wife, her mannerisms were not correct. The feelings he usually had when close to her were not there, and there seemed to be a lack of the usual emotions. Nevertheless, it looked like her, and it was beyond his reasoning to stop.

As the act climaxed, the subject closed his eyes. When it was over, he opened his eyes to find that it wasn't his wife at all. The figure was now a gray alien being.

He jumped back and demanded to know why she did that to him.

The alien looked confused by his reaction. She explained that she felt he was very lonely and she wanted to make him happy.

The subject said he realized that the gray thought she was doing the right thing and could not seem to comprehend why he was upset by it.

Event 16
Subject: Adult Male
Date: 1995
Location: United States

(Comment: This event is a good illustration of the aliens' apparent lack of understanding concerning the difference some humans have between love and sex. Though the subject in this event is a gay man, we do not believe his sexual preference was the issue in this event at all. It appears that the aliens were trying to understand the difference between his deep love for the woman in the event, in contrast to his lack of sexual want for her.

It must be noted that we have collected many examples like the one below. They crossed all sexual preference groups.

On occasion, people have reported they engaged in an arranged sexual encounter in the alien environment, even though the encounter was something they would never even consider in their earth-life. This must send mixed messages to the aliens as they try to sort out human sexual behavior. That is, assuming sorting out human sexual behavior is what they are doing.

Consider that they may be trying to allow each individual exposed to these types of events the forum to explore their own sexuality in ways they would not in the constraints of their earth-life. Also consider the following explanation some people received from the aliens. They were told that sexual contact causes an energy exchange, and that the point of these encounters is the energy of the person, not the sex of the body the person is in.)

The subject reported being in the company of the aliens. The grays brought him to a room where a close friend of his was sitting. The friend was a woman about his same age. The beings asked him why he never had sex with her, and asked him if he wanted to have sex with her now. The woman seemed to be fine with the idea.

He tried to explain to the grays that he was a homosexual and though he loved this woman dearly, he didn't want to have a sexual encounter with her or any other woman.

The aliens didn't seem to understand. They asked him to sit there and wait a moment, then they walked out. After they walked out, his friend came over to him and started to become sexually forward with him. The subject explained that it not only bothered him because of his sexual preference, but also because he felt his friend was being coerced

She began to tell him how she secretly loved him. He pushed her away and she began to cry. The subject said he felt like the only way to stop his friend's hurt was to give in to her sexual advancements. Despite his pain over seeing her cry, he couldn't bring himself to do it.

The subject reported he sat for some time, struggling with the conflict between his want to make his friend happy and stop her pain, and his own feelings.

After a short time, the alien returned and asked him why he didn't have sex with his friend, even though he knew how much she loved him and how badly she wanted to have sex with him.

The alien asked why humans will often have sex with people they don't love, but will not necessarily have sex with people they love dearly.

The subject tried to explain that love and sex were not the same thing. He reported that he believed the being did not understand him.

Event 17
Subject: Adult Female
Date: 1997
Location: United States

(Comment: The following two events illustrate examples of times when the aliens' apparently tried to fool a subject into having a sexual encounter against her will.

In the first event the subject reported she believed the grays did not understand they did anything wrong to her.)

The subject reported that she was in the middle of an abduction event. She was asked by the gray aliens and a tall human looking alien to enter a room and wait for someone.

After a short time, another person walked into the room. It was an actor from a television show she loved.

The man walked up to her and started to caress and kiss her. At first she didn't want him to touch her, but for reasons she could not explain, she gave into his advances and began to enjoy the encounter.

This particular actor had thick, curly hair. She reached up to touch his hair. This was something she always dreamed of doing as his fan. The subject reported that something felt strange about the man's hair. It wasn't thick and curly. It was rather thin, straight and very short.

She began to wonder why she could see something, but feel something else. She reported that she began to find other discrepancies between what she saw and what her hands were touching. She asked what was going on. The person's voice said, "Don't worry about it. Just relax."

She knew that the voice didn't match that of the actor's. Moreover, the voice was female. She tried to push the person off, but couldn't because she kept slipping back into the illusion that it was the actor she wanted to be with.

The subject gave into the event and continued to be intimate with the other person. The person with her performed oral sex on her and after the act was over, she was able to break the screen and realized that she was, in fact, with another woman. The subject became enraged and embarrassed. She started to cry.

Two gray beings came into the room. One led the other woman out. The second gray asked the subject why she was upset. The being didn't understand why she was angry, since she obviously sexually enjoyed the event. He asked her, "Why is the pleasure you experienced no longer pleasure?"

She tried to explain and the gray said, "Isn't pleasure always pleasure?"

He explained that the energy of the pleasure changed when she realized what happened, but the physical pleasure should have remained the same.

The subject reported she became very frustrated and stopped trying to explain.

Event 18
Subject: Adult Female
Date: 1995
Location: United States

(Comment: In this event, the subject reported she was able to break out of the illusion and stop the encounter. When you read the explanation the alien gives the subject for the event, consider that it might be the truth. If it is, and the gray wanted to make the woman in the event happy, wouldn't it be easier to create an illusion of the subject for the woman? If the explanation about energy is the truth, this inconsistency could be explained.)

The subject was abducted by a group of gray aliens. They were doing some kind of procedure to her. She didn't know what they were doing. After they were done, they led the subject into a room. She knew it was a room and had walls, but there was a stream and trees in the room.

The subject sat on a rock in the stream and dangled her feet in the water. She started to feel "dreamy". She noticed a person come in. He looked like a beautiful human man. The man paid a lot of physical attention to her, and began to fondle her.

The subject reported that the disoriented feeling got stronger and stronger. As it did, the person she was with started to change in appearance. His looks ranged from that of a boy in high school she once had a crush on, to an actor she believed to be sexy, and many faces in between.

She began to give into the event and slipped into the feeling that it was a very pleasurable dream. While they touched each other, she reached down to the man's genitals only to find that he didn't have any. She realized that there was something wrong. She then started to break the screen memory. Though she was seeing bulging muscles, she was feeling slim, feminine arms.

Finally, she was able to fight the dream-like state to find that she was being intimate with a woman. This truly bothered her because of her heterosexual preference. What made matters worse, was that the woman she found herself with was a woman she once worked with in her earth-life. The two of them were close friends, but the friendship fell apart after the woman expressed her sexual feelings for the subject.

The subject broke away from the woman and ran out of the room, only to be stopped by a taller gray being. She demanded to know why they tricked her into having sex with this woman. The gray explained that he wanted to make the woman happy, and asked the subject if it was so much to ask of her to make the other woman happy. He went on to explain that it was such a small inconvenience to the subject, but meant so much to the other woman.

Section 2
Community

It may seem like a new concept to some readers and indeed even to some researchers, but alien created communities of human subjects have existed for a long time. Many lifelong experiencers have numerous and vivid memories of their interactions in this alien created world.

As stated before, this side of the phenomena seldom, if ever, gets media attention. This is because it is so amazing to believe — even for those who have come so far as to believe in alien abduction to begin with — that it is beyond the paradigm of most people. Nevertheless, this aspect of the contact phenomena is very real and undeniable. The number of stories and the consistency of those stories are a testament to this fact.

It was a difficult task for us to decide which events to offer you, the reader. There were many, and most were similar in the overall theme with respect to the community. Still, just as it is in our human lives, each individual report of their interactions with the alien structured community varies with the person's exact experience and their perception.

When setting up categories to illustrate examples we settled on those listed below for the following reasons:

• **ET Schools:** It is common for all contactees who interact in these communities to be involved with ET schools, whether as a student, teacher, or both.

+ **Community Interactions:** In this section you will find examples of common occurrences that illustrate interaction between people in a community setting.

+ **Celebrities:** Another common occurrence for people interacting in the alien community is apparent interaction with human celebrities.

+ **Spiritual Experiences:** Just as with ET schools, just about all in the alien community are involved with — or exposed to — spiritual experiences that can be profoundly life changing when they are recalled.

The alien-based community of experiencers is going to become an increasingly prominent force in the future of abduction research and help. With the aid of such things as the Internet, people from the alien-based community are finding one another at breakneck speed. It is truly changing more than the study of UFOlogy. It is changing the world.

As people with like experiences come together and realize that their memories of an ET community are real, they move forward in search of the individuals they know from this community. They are finding them.

This is a strong tool in building the validity of individuals experiencing alien contact.

At one time, all an experiencer had was a handful of books and articles about medical experiments and nighttime kidnapping for reference. They were forced to look to a few over-worked professionals and the slanted views of the media for their sense of confirmation and validity.

Imagine the freedom and sense of home these people are experiencing when they can sign onto the Internet and find a person they have been sharing experiences with all their life. The sense of empowerment and freedom is immeasurable.

These types of meetings are documented, yet the media, by and large, have chosen to ignore these accounts.

Everyone is talking about finding a *smoking gun*. Everyone is asking, "Why don't they fly over the White House?"

The fact is, we have been given more than one *smoking gun*, but the public ignored them. There have even been mass sightings over Washington DC. None of which have proven to the world that aliens are real, or that people who have contact are telling the truth.

It appears it is going to be the way the abductees have been saying it is for years. It appears that the undeniable proof is only going to come from the people.

As more and more contactees remember the community and find people they have shared lives with while there, they find the proof of their own experiences and the self confidence to disregard those who hope to discredit them and mute their messages.

As people recall the alien community, they work to find those they remember. When they do, they recreate that community here on Earth.

This, above all, is a compelling reason why we, the human race, can no longer afford to turn our back on this phenomena.

Section 2.1 ET Schools

In this section we are going to explore events that took place in school rooms in the alien community. People consistently describe these school rooms as looking very much like human schools, with desks, chairs and pencils.

In the creation of these schools, it appears the aliens invested a lot of time and effort to make sure they created an environment that made their human subjects comfortable.

Seldom do people report having classes in rooms that are alien-like, with white curving walls. Nevertheless, many remember being taught lessons that were far beyond anything one would learn in a human school.

What is taught in the ET schools? Most report that they are taught concepts of universal spiritualism, psychic exercises, advanced physics and survival techniques.

Knowing that the aliens have an ability to accurately see the future (see Event 11) are they training their community of human subjects to survive in a time when there will be no modern conveniences? Are they teaching them skills they will need to use after that time has passed?

Many contactees believe they are doing just that. Like it or not, these people are convinced they are being trained not only to survive in a time of turmoil, but they are also being taught what they will need to know in order to rebuild the world after the turmoil is over.

What will this new world be like? It is said to be one of truth and love. Many believe this, many do not. Regardless of what any individual believes it will be like, most agree it will happen. The ET schools are preparing contactees for it.

Event 19
Subject: Adult Female
Date: 1995
Location: United States

(Comment: This is a typical example of one type of memory common among people who teach in ET schools. It is very common for subjects to know exactly what they are teaching with great clarity, but to forget all the technical details upon their return home.

Why would the aliens have a need to take such time and make such effort to teach humans these things if there was not a need for it? When you consider the theory of all these events being some kind of experiment on the aliens' part, you must also consider the vast amount of resources that consistently go into these types of school events and how long they have continued.)

The subject was brought into a human looking classroom by a gray alien being. He told her to teach the people there about the items that were resting on the teacher's desk. Which she did.

At the time, she knew that each item on the desk was some kind of tool that humans needed to master the use of in order to survive after the time of *Earth changes* the aliens talk about. She picked up each one, and asked people to come up and tell everyone what it was and how it worked. She reported that she knew exactly what each item did and how to use it, but by the time she got home she did not recall anything about them.

After a while, she picked up some kind of instrument and walked around each person in the room. As she passed it over each person's head, the instrument gave a reading by projecting a colored strip across a scale on the face of the instrument. The subject recorded both the reading on the scale and the color it turned for the whole class of approximately eighteen people.

Event 20
Subject: Teenaged Female
Date: 1978
Location: United States

(Comment: This example shows that school is school no matter where you are. Often, when we think of alien run classes, we are tempted to think of them as being perfectly quiet and organized, as if they were taught by and filled with robots. It appears they are not.)

The subject reported she was sitting in what looked exactly like a human high school. There was a boy sitting in front of her who she liked a lot. The teacher standing in the front of the room wasn't human. He was a gray alien. He was talking, but his mouth was not moving.

She stretched out and put her bare feet though an opening in the back of the chair in front of her and under the boy's bottom. She started to poke his bottom with her toes, trying to tease and distract him.

The subject pointed out that she would never do this to a boy in her Earth high school. But for some reason, she felt it was fine to do there.

The boy turned around and told her to stop, but she did not. She reported that she was having fun teasing him.

The alien at the front of the room told her to stop it. She did, but only for a minute, then started again.

She said the alien came over and looked her in the eyes. He said, "You are being bad." Then he touched the subject and she could no longer move her feet until class was over.

The subject added that she did not pay attention to the topic being taught in the class at all. Rather, she pouted about having her feet paralyzed.

Upon returning home, she was angry at herself for not paying attention. But at the time she thought the subject was so boring that she did not listen.

Event 21
Subject: Adult Male
Date: 1998
Location: Canada

(Comment: Once again, the subject knew things — in this case a foreign language — but could not recall it upon his return .

Many contactees report they have been taught to speak a foreign language by the aliens. Some contactees, who are multilingual, report they are sure it is not an Earth language, yet it appears to have a common root to the romantic languages of Europe, such as French and Spanish and it is far removed from the language of clicks and hisses many contactees report hearing the gray aliens speak among themselves. What advantage is there for the aliens to teach all contactees a common tongue?

As we know, language links culture and community. One common tongue unites all abductees, no matter what their mother tongue.)

The subject reported in this abduction, just like many others he had experienced before, he found himself sitting in a classroom with a group of people. In this instance, he was sitting in a front corner of the room. There were a number of people who appeared to be in their late teens and early twenties sitting in chairs that looked just like the type used in human schools. The classroom looked like a normal, human classroom.

At the front of the room was a gentleman approximately forty years old. He was clearly in charge. Everyone was speaking in a language that was not English. During the experience, the subject reported that he understood what was being said and what was going on.

The teacher said something and pointed to a young man who was sitting in the corner of the room, opposite to the subject. This man began by saying a one syllable word, then the person behind him said another single syllable, and the next person did the same, so on down the rows of students. It was as if each person in the classroom was sounding out a letter of an alphabet in some foreign language. The subject said they started going faster until they were doing it at an incredibly fast speed.

He sat there, listening intently, and calculating what word would come next. When the subject's turn came, he knew he was going to have to say something very specific and in a certain pattern or accent. He was the last person in the room, and it appeared to the subject that he was expected to know something special.

The subject reported that at that time he understood the very odd, foreign language as if it were his own native tongue.

When he was returned home, he remembered the experience, but could not remember the translation of the language.

Event 22
Subject: Adult Male
Date: 1999
Location: United Kingdom

(Comment: Telepathy during ET school is very common. So is the 'buzzing effect', as well as the out-of-body feeling described in this event.

What is not described here, but just as common, is a feeling of joining with the others in the room, once the out-of-body effect occurs. Again, this mixing of souls and energy creates a bonding between the contactees involved.

Why bother to go to such extents to bond individuals and create a community if the objective is to study and breed people like lab rats?)

The subject reported finding himself sitting in what seemed like a human classroom, but the teacher was not human. The teacher was a gray alien. No one spoke anything out loud. All the communication between teacher and students was done on a telepathic level.

There was some kind of a drill going on. Each student was chosen, in turn, by the gray teacher to say a word that was telepathically transmitted to them by the alien. The subject was intent on getting it right and was concentrating with all his strength.

The pace of the drill got faster and louder until each person chosen was shouting out their answer at the top of their lungs.

The feeling in the room became charged and the subject felt like he was beginning to spin, even though he was sitting still. The drill went on until the subject reported that he felt like he was no longer in his body, but had been swept up in the furry of energy that was buzzing around the room.

Event 23
Subject: Adult Male
Date: 1998
Location: United Kingdom

(Comment: Not everyone who finds his or herself in an alien classroom believes it is real. Because abductions can sometimes have a dream-like aura, abductees occasionally believe they are actually dreaming

This could be a human coping device for a situation the individual cannot fit into their paradigm, rather than an alien ploy to fool people. If it were an alien ploy, why are the other five people in the room aware of where they are?)

The subject reported he was sitting in a classroom that looked human-made, during an alien encounter. He was asked by the aliens to sit with a small group of six adults and talk to them as if he were their teacher. He said the point of his being there was more to keep an eye on the people than to actually teach them anything.

The classroom was described as being small, painted a dull, light gray and having the bottom of a staircase built into the wall and roof on one side, as if the schoolroom was created in the small space under a stairwell. He was seated near where the ceiling came down, and found that he bumped his head if he were not careful.

The people in the class were sitting, facing the subject and they were talking about physics, wormholes and folding time. Everything they were talking about was very informal. Everyone was speculating as to what the nature of such things were.

One woman in the class started to make strange, guttural sounds.

"What are you doing?" the subject asked the student.

"This is my dream. I will do what I wish," the woman replied.

The subject suggested she keep quiet as the rest of them were having a discussion, but the woman did not stop. She started to groan and make animal-like noises. Then she got up from her chair and started dancing around the room singing, "It's my dream and I'll do what I want."

The subject was very annoyed. He reported that he wanted to continue to talk to the group about the science topics, but the woman was too distracting.

Not long after, a gray alien entered the room and they were all taken away. This is where his memory ends.

Event 24
Subject: Michelle
Date: 1995
Location: United States

(Comment: This event shows how the alien schools use stories and activities to reinforce ideas, much in the same way human schools do. This strongly suggest that the focus is student learning, rather than ET experimentation.)

I was woken up by an ET and told that I had to go with him and work. I got up, and the room filled with blue light. I found myself moving, without walking, into the blue light as if it was sucking me into it. I was brought on shipboard where I was told to go into a small room that had a low table and a strange panel of instruments on the far wall. I sat on the table and a small gray being holding a device, that looked like a miniature model of the Sidney Opera House, came up to me and waved the device over my body. There was a strange tingly feeling where it passed.

After this quick scanning, Hetar came in and told me my assignment for that visit was to teach a group of human children the working of triangles. He instructed me as to what room I would find them in. I nodded my understanding and walked away.

The room was down a curving hallway and on my right. I walked in to find a group of about twenty children who all appeared to be ten to twelve years old sitting quietly waiting. The room was set up very much like a human schoolroom. The desk and chairs were typical of an American classroom. The teacher's desk looked the same as well. There was even a blackboard behind the teacher's desk.

I recognized several of the children from other work I had done with them, but couldn't tell you more than a few first names. We began our session and I told them they were going to learn about triangles.

I passed out five-inch squares of thick paper to each of them. The paper was red on one side and yellow on the other.

I began to tell them a story. As I spoke, I folded my own paper in a particular way and instructed each of them to do the same. In the end, when the story was completed, we each had made our own version of a strange, four-pointed object that looked a bit like a *cootie catcher* children make in grade school. But it was different from that.

After we were done, we attached each of our own objects with those of the other children to form a huge ball that expanded and contracted. Then we played with the ball as a class.

I know I have done this exercise many times with many groups of children. Yet, to this day, I cannot fully recall the story I tell as I fold the paper. However, I do recall it has something to do with the way triangles bend and something to do with being able to make all shapes with triangles.

Though I don't remember the story, I recall exactly how to fold the object.

Event 25
Subject: Adult Female
Date: On going
Location: United States

(Comment: Survival arts seem to be an important part of ET school. People are taught not just how to survive such things as nuclear explosions or wars, but also how to feed themselves and make or find the necessities of life

The following event indicates that the Earth may be destined to once again become a hunter/gatherer society.)

The subject, who is a Native American Elder, reported that she has many memories of being abducted by the gray beings, and brought into a classroom-like setting to teach.

She reported that the theme of the classes she teaches is survival arts. She teaches human students of all ages and nationalities to do things such as, make baskets from grasses, identify and prepare roots and plants for food, make natural medicines from herbs and even skin and prepare animals for eating.

When asked how she does these things in an alien environment, such as an ET base or ship, the subject explained that all the supplies she needs are provided for her. She said they are always there, in the classroom when she arrives.

We were particularly surprised about the animal carcasses, since many contactees feel their alien contacts compel them to not eat meat or kill animals. We were also curious about where the aliens got animal carcasses.

She said she didn't know where they got them, but she suspected that they were not real, but rather some kind of synthetic equivalent. She based this assumption on how quickly they could be cleaned, dried and tanned. She said it was as if they were examples created for her to be able to show the whole process in a short period of time.

The subject explained that her ancestral people find these arts an important part of human life. Even in a *new world,* humans would be less than what the Earth wanted them to be if these skills were taken away from all people. She said she is sure the aliens know this and that is why they are teaching some people these skills.

Section 2.2 Community Interactions

Like all communities, the one that exists in the alien environment is varied and growing. Many people remember having friends, relationships, and whole other lives there. Many more recall bits and pieces of their experiences in the alien created community.

Because events that happen in the community seldom, if ever, fit into the standard medical template expected by most abduction researchers, people who report such interactions are usually disregarded.

Also, because the community is a fully functional community, and the relationships there are very real, occasionally a person will report some kind of personal conflict in this community. When these events are reported the contactee is usually regarded as having some kind of Earth-based emotional issues he is working out in his dreams.

In fact, many contactees find community memories so difficult to assimilate, they are far more likely to label them as dreams, regardless of how clear their recall and how factual the event.

When we examine this closer, it often appears that people with community memories long to be with their non-earth-based friends. Many of them have strong love relationships there. Often these relationships are stronger than those they may have with their Earth spouses. Memories of friendships from the alien-based community become very real as people explore and recall more and more of these events.

Thanks to such things as the Internet, the number of people who have been able to find others they know from the alien community grows each year. This is helping contactees, who otherwise struggle with feelings of loneliness and isolation, to feel complete and comfortable.

Most of the community-based events we received from contactees were about their personal interactions with people they knew while in the community. Almost all of these reflected the subject's strong love for the person, as well as their need to find them here on Earth. Although these events are important to each individual for obvious reasons, and important to all of us, because the structure of the world around us changes with every contactee who works to recreate that community here on Earth, they truly can be summed up as they have been in Event 28.

Instead, we have chosen to give you examples of people's interactions with the community that were just as valid, common to several different sources, but not specific to the individual's personal life.

We believe you will find them an interesting and revealing look into the world of the ET community.

Event 26
Subject: Child Male
Date: 1962
Location: United Kingdom

(Comment: The event that follows is typical of this type of contact. In reported events such as this, the subjects were contacted as children and asked to do a job, help the animals of the world, or in this case, help babies. It is a common thread in the alien community to start teaching children from an early age that they are here to help others.

Also, notice the statement made by the alien about the creation of the babies. This report correlates with several sources we have that indicate the production of halfling children [hybrids] is not the intention of the aliens work here on Earth.)

The subject was ten years old. He was outside riding his bicycle alone. He said that his mother didn't like him to ride his bike alone because she was afraid that he would fall into one of the many waterways in the town. As he was riding, he saw something that caught his eye. It was a bright light. He went down an alley way toward the light. The light seemed to rush toward him. He tried to outrun it, but couldn't. It overtook him and he found himself lying on a hard, cold table.

After he came to, a gray alien being, who was shorter then he was, led him into a room that was filled with little children who were playing on the floor. They were very young. The subject believed the babies to be between a year and two years old at most.

The subject asked the gray, "Did you kidnap all those children?"

The gray replied telepathically, "Of course not. We made them, but we don't know what to do with them."

The subject asked, "Why would you make them if you don't know what to do with them?"

The alien replied, "We didn't make them on purpose. Now we have to learn what to do with them. We need people to help them." The alien then asked the subject if he wanted to help them.

The subject asked how he could help the babies, and the alien replied that he just had to love them. "You can love, can't you?" the gray asked.

The subject replied, "Yes, I can love. I think so."

The gray said, "Practice that. Then you can love and you will do it unconditionally."

The subject reported that at that point, the light faded and he found himself sitting on his bicycle. He headed home to find that hours had passed and his mother was so afraid he fell into a canal or waterway that she had called the police.

Event 27
Subject: Child Female (as told by mother)
Date: 1997
Location: United States

(Comment: The child in the next event was far too young to do any research on the topic she talked about. She could not even read.

This is a good example of the apparent training of children to take on certain roles in the future by alien visitors.)

The subject's mother was making breakfast for her children when her two-year-old daughter got up and came into the kitchen. She told her mother that she had been visited by the "little doctor people" the night before. The mother, knowing that she, herself, was a contactee, was not totally surprised that her child was also. Nevertheless, she was concerned. She asked her daughter what happened.

The child, who was twenty-eight months old, went on to explain to her mother that the little doctor people took her out of her bed and made her fly with them to China. She said they showed her how many people lived in China. She explained to her mother that the aliens told her when she was older she would have to work in China. It would be a time when the people of China would be hungry and they would want to eat the biggest and best vegetables, corn and wheat, but she would have to teach them that they should eat the smallest and have to save the biggest and best for planting again next year. If they did not save the biggest and best for planting, every year the plants would be smaller and smaller until there would not be enough food for everyone.

Her mother asked her what television show she had learned that from. The child was adamant that the *little doctor people* told her when they brought her to China while her mother was asleep.

Event 28
Subject: Adult Female
Date: 1997
Location: United States

(Comment: Although this event happened at some kind of cosmic bus stop setting, what happened there is typical of the types of events people in the alien community are experiencing and the promises they are making to find each other here on Earth. They are keeping these promises in greater numbers each year.)

The subject reported she was standing at a strange bus stop. She said she knew it was in a place the aliens often took her because she remembered being there several times before. On other occasions she saw the gray aliens there as well. This time there were no aliens present.

She described the buses as not being normal. She said they looked like buses at first, but there was something wrong with them. After much staring, she realized they had no tires.

The subject reported that most of the time when she was at this bus stop it was to greet human people who were getting off the incoming buses. But this time she was there because she was going to meet with someone to say good-bye, and then board a bus herself.

The man she was waiting for walked over. He was with two small gray beings. She described him as a small man, not much taller than herself. Although she did not find him physically attractive, she said there was something about him she found irresistible. She knew that he was a very important person in her life and that she loved him very much.

She hugged him and said goodbye. But she did not want to let him go. She said to him that someday she would find him in human life. He agreed that he would do everything he could to find her. The bus came and she got in, leaving the man behind.

When she returned to her home, she recalled the man's face and her love for him. She was, at the time of this writing, actively looking for this man her on Earth.

Event 29
Subject: Michelle
Date: 1978
Location: United States

(Comment: This event, although not completely typical of contactee behavior, illustrates a friendship relationship between Michelle and another teen on shipboard.

Notice the behavior of the crowd waiting for the aliens to come. Though there was a sense of mild fear among them, that fear was far less than one would imagine it should be under such circumstances. Could this be because the people knew they were not truly in any danger, thus their "fight or flight" instincts were not aroused?

This event raises the question; why do Michelle and her friend remember, when the others in the room do not?)

I was on shipboard talking to a friend I saw there rather often. Her name was Theresa. She was from the southern United States. I saw her many times when I was a teen. We talked about boys, what a pain our little brothers were, school and all the other typical things teens talked about.

She and I had quite a bit of freedom on shipboard. We were allowed to run around the decks and do what we pleased, within reason.

The day of this event in particular, we were picked up with a group of about 20 people. They were not all from the same place. Although I believe we were all from the North American continent. We were collected one by one and assembled in a room to wait for the aliens to come and get us.

Of all the contact events I had, this type of event happened about four times a year. When it did, Theresa and I were always collected with the same group of people. Aside from us, the group consisted of several middle aged men and woman, a few older teens or young adults, two elderly ladies and one outspoken boy who seemed to be about twelve.

We were always made to wait in the same room. It was round and about twenty feet across. It had a ladder-like set of steps built into the wall that led to a catwalk around the top of the room. The ledge was at least fifteen feet from the floor and was rimmed with a black metal railing.

Theresa and I climbed up the ladder and onto the catwalk. We sat there with our legs dangling down into the room below. We felt we were so very cool as we sat up there and laughed at the people in the room at our feet.

For some reason, each time we were gathered together the others would have no memory of being brought together before, though they knew they were with aliens.

After so many times, Theresa and I knew that every time the group was brought together, they would work to devise some kind of plan to overtake or subdue the ETs.

We sat there on the ledge of the room and bet with each other as to what approach they would take this time. Would they agree to have some of the bigger guys hide against the wall by the door and jump the ETs when they came through the door again? Would they try to bargain with the ETs again? Would they declare their human rights again? We bantered back and forth and laughed at the people.

The young boy in the group suggested that if they gave up to the ETs and begged them not to harm them, maybe they could talk to them. A middle aged man who was dressed in a plaid flannel shirt suggested that if they were submissive to the ETs as the boy suggested they could explain to them that they were not going to hurt the ETs and they were welcome to come in peace. An elderly woman suggested that if they prayed to the ETs maybe they would treat them nicely. Someone even suggested asking the aliens for political asylum.

The people all talked about what they were going to do, but Theresa and I knew exactly what was going to happen no matter what they planned. The doors were going to slide open. The ETs would come in, and the people would do nothing but stand there, like they did every time.

That was exactly what happened. The door opened and the people just stood there silently as a large group of little gray beings came into the room and took each person by the arm and led them into the next room.

Theresa and I laughed and teased as the people were led away. At sixteen years old, she and I both thought the people were hilarious. After all, we had control. We didn't turn into zombies when aliens were around. We gave each other a "high-five" and smiled.

The room emptied leaving only Hetar standing in the doorway. He looked up at both of us sitting on the catwalk, then motioned with his finger for us to come down. I said to my friend, "Time to pay for the ride."

She laughed, then we climbed down and hurried to Hetar's side.

Event 30
Subject: Adult Woman
Date: 1998
Location: United States

(Comment: This event is a good example of how people comfort each other and work together in the community. Also, notice the exchange of energy. Though it is not something we go into great detail about, it is a fact that much of the central theme of alien interactions, in and out of the community setting, has to do with the exchange of energy [psychic or soul based]. This energy can be used to heal, comfort and strengthen.)

The subject reported that she was abducted by gray aliens. She was feeling very upset. Someone in her family was very sick and she felt they were going to die soon. When the aliens came to get her, she was crying and carrying on. She didn't want them to bother her and was mad at them because she expected them to cure her sick relative, which they did not.

She reported she was very angry and refused to do anything they wanted her to do. One of them told her that he wanted her to go and think about things for a while. He led her to a ladder. She climbed up it to a hatch in the ceiling, then pushed on the hatch and it opened. She went inside and the hatch closed behind her.

She reported that the room was completely round with a column in the center. The walls were curved and the floor was the only thing flat in the whole place. The walls were bright white, but she didn't see where the light was coming from. Because of the center column in the middle, she described it as if she were standing inside a donut shape.

She walked around the circle of the donut. It made her feel dizzy. When she got about half way around, she saw a human man sitting on a blanket on the floor. He was someone she knew, but she had not seen him in a long time. He had grown a beard. He told her to sit down. She did.

He said that he was there to help her deal with her pain. He told her that he wanted to take her pain away, but she didn't want him to because she thought it would make him feel bad. He touched her and she started to cry and tell him about her sick relative. After some time, he asked her if she were feeling better. They started to talk about his life. He told her that he just bought a new motor home and was planning to go on a trip across the country.

After a while, he said it was time to go and he picked up the blanket. She helped him fold it and they walked to the hatch and climbed back down the ladder. When they got to the bottom, there was a gray being waiting for them. The alien asked her if she was feeling better and she nodded. He then led her back to the room she started in.

The next day she reported that she called the man from the event. She said he does not believe in aliens, never mind thinks he is an abductee. Though she had not seen him in several years, he said it was funny that she called when she did, because he had been thinking about her for the first time in years.

She asked him if he grew a beard, and he said he did. She then asked him if he just bought a motor home and once again he said he did.

THE BRIDGE

The following two accounts come from Michelle and Paul's lives. They were recorded many years before the pair met here on Earth, and are an example of the community at work.

There are foreshadows of a future event in these tellings, as well as indications that the aliens have trained various professionals to take over communities when and if this time of *Earth Changes* happens.

Keep in mind as you read the following two accounts, neither Paul nor Michelle knew each other here on Earth at the time of the event.

Event: 31
Subject: Michelle
Date: 1992
Location: United States
(Comment: This happened not long before the breakup of Michelle's marriage. Some of the issues discussed involved that decision. Those issues will not be included in this event for privacy reasons.)

I was sitting up in bed, awake, thinking about a decision I had to make surrounding the state of my life and marriage. George (my then husband) had been very difficult and I was struggling with issues.

A female gray ET came in the room and asked me to go with her. She told me that they were taking George with them as well. We were transported to the ship on a beam of blue light. We entered a waiting area and I was told to go upstairs to an area where others were assembled.

George followed me. We went up a flight of stairs and entered a room at the top. It was a small room with benches around it that came out of the wall itself, making it seem like a molded hot tub.

George sat down and I sat to his left. There were several people standing around the room. They were all human. I recognized most of them. A few of them were actually regulars at a support group I attended on Earth at the time. It was quiet and people were just standing around chatting peacefully.

A smaller gray being entered. He called everyone to order and began to make a speech.

Like a bolt of lightening, a human man came bounding up the stairs. The small gray stopped talking and waited for the man to take his seat. The man had striking blue eyes. I knew that I knew him very well, but for some reason, when I returned home, I couldn't place him. He pushed gently by me to sit down. As he did, he touched my shoulder in a friendly way. He nodded hello to George and sat on beside him.

George leaned over to me and demanded, "Do you know him!"

I was sure I knew him, but I didn't want to tell George that I did. So I said, "Maybe. I'm not sure."

The man was dressed in a well pressed pair of jeans and a nice shirt. The rest of us were in the more 'standard issue' hospital gown-like outfits the ETs sometime give us on board.

The moderator started to speak again. The man cleared this throat and broke in, "Excuse me, but could I interrupt?" he said. The moderator nodded.

The man said, "Hi George! Hi Michelle! How have you been?" Then he got up and sat right between George and me. He turned his back to me and started to talk to George.

The man shifted himself and then put his arm around me. I felt very comfortable in his arm, even with my husband right there. Nevertheless, it did feel awkward.

Even though the moderator was speaking, George and the man kept talking to each other. They became louder and louder until their talking disrupted the room. George seemed to be getting more and more restless. The other man seemed very comfortable. He even seemed a bit arrogant about the whole thing.

Finally, the man realized it was bothering the speaker and said, "Come on, let's go someplace quiet to talk."

He led George and I out of the room. We followed him down the hall. As we walked he held my hand. It did not feel odd at all. George followed close behind. He did not seem to mind that the man was holding my hand. He did not appear angered or jealous one bit.

We sat at a table in a small, but long room. The man crossed one leg over the other and then leaned his chair back, balancing it on its back legs. He and George started to talk again. Neither man was talking to me. They sat sitting facing each other and I was sitting off to the side on George's left and the man's right.

I listened as the man talked sternly with George. He told George that he was not taking care of me properly. He said that I was important to some mission and that George knew that when he took the job of taking care of me from him (the man). With all this talk, I started to feel like an child or an object, without a say in things. I wanted to speak out about it, but the man and George didn't give me a chance to get a word in. The man continued to point out to George the things he was doing that were hurting me both physically and emotionally.

George was getting increasingly more annoyed with the man. Still, it was hard for me to really care. After all, it was the truth and I had wanted to say those things to George for years, but could not.

I started to think about my life and drifted off into a daydream world of my own. I was not really paying attention to what they were saying anymore. Perhaps it was too hard for me to listen to it all in my current emotional state at the time. George kept getting all worked up until he was really upset. He began to shout. When he did, the man said things to calm him. Then their discussion would start all over again.

I really don't know how many times this happened because I wasn't paying much attention. I was thinking about the man. In the middle of their conversation, I interrupted and asked him, "When did you shave your mustache and beard?"

He smiled and touched his clean face then said, "When you told me you'd didn't like..." He stopped mid-sentence and glared at George.

The man started to talk to George again. He continued to bring George to the point of rage then make him calm down. Finally the man said, "This is getting us no where." He reached over and took my hand. "Come on. I want to talk to you," he said. He stood up and motioned for me to go with him.

George also stood up. But now George looked different. He seemed to be in a sudden trance.

"What about him?" I asked.

A little gray being walked up behind George and led him away.

"Don't worry. They will take him home before I get you back there," he said. We both watched for moment longer as the alien led George away, then we walked down the hall in the opposite direction.

We walked to a room that was darkly lit. It seemed to have some strange kind of desk in it and some large containers that I thought were storage boxes. There was a round spot on the floor that was dark gray in color. We stood on the spot and the next thing I was aware of was standing outside on the Earth's surface. The man was standing at my side.

It was night. The air was warm and slightly damp like it had rained recently. It was the end of November and snow covered everything in New England, where I lived, so I knew we were no where near there.

From where we were standing, we had our backs to a large chain link fence. Behind it was a brick building sitting in the dark of some dim parking lot lights.

The setting was familiar to me. I mentioned this to him and he said I knew the place but for reasons he would explain later, I didn't remember it.

We began to walk and I remembered what I was wearing. I became concerned that someone would see us and think something was wrong, because I was still dressed in the clothes the ETs provided for me and must have looked like I walked out of a human hospital, bear feet and all.

He pointed to the sky and I saw a big, black, triangle shaped craft hovering silently above us. It was a strange feeling.

We talked about my life as we walked the dark streets. I was so confused. I knew I had known this man all my life and I had very strong emotions for him, but I couldn't even remember his name. Yet I felt comfortable enough to tell him even my deepest secrets and concerns. Moreover, he seemed to already know all about it. When I asked him why, he said it was because we talked about it before, I just didn't remember it.

He told me he loved me, that he always did, and always will. He said that he would always be there to take care of me and that he was there now because he promised that he would always be there when I really needed him. He promised that soon he would be with me in my human life and things would be better.

I told him I hoped he would, because I could not live without him. He smiled and said, "You will find me soon. Don't worry."

Our walk led us down a few small streets then up a grassy hill to a highway. It seemed odd, but there were no cars around. We walked down the shoulder of the highway until we came to a bridge that spanned a great distance across an open canyon with a river running through it. In the distance there was a dam. It was wider than it was tall and it had sodium lights on it, so that it was bathed in a beautiful orange light. It was an awesome sight to see. The vision of it embedded in my mind and I know I will recognize it if I see it again.

There were people sitting on a metal conduit on one side of the bridge. There was no sidewalk. This was a bridge for cars only. One of the people was a middle-aged woman with short, straight, black hair and bangs. I remember calling her Patty. There were two men sitting next to her. One was named David. I know this because the woman called him by name. David had dark wavy hair and a round, pleasant face. The man that sat on the other side was thin and gave the impression of being very tall. He had almost curly blond hair and a very long sharp-featured face. There were others behind them, but I couldn't really see them in the dark.

I asked, "What is this place?"

Everyone looked at me as if I said something amusing.

The man I was with said, "Go easy on her. She going through her time of purging now and doesn't remember. She is having a really hard time of things because of George on top of that."

The woman smirked and said, "Not George again!"

The man hugged me and said, "We'll get her through despite him. Might even get him through in the process."

Oddly, I didn't think to ask what my *time of purging* was all about and when it was going to be over.

We talked about George for a short while. Finally I asked again, "What is this place?"

"This is our place," the woman answered. "The place where we will be when it's time. This is our place," she said again as if I should understand.

We talked about the changes that were coming to the world and I got upset. I asked her, "How can you be so excited and happy about this stuff? Millions of people are going to suffer and die."

"You're not understanding," the woman explained. "You are thinking of death as an end. It is not. Nothing dies, it transforms."

I wanted to say something like, "Remember that when you're on your death bed!" But I held my tongue. I knew it wouldn't be well received.

We talked for a while longer. The sun was starting to come up. The man said, "They say it's time to go. "

I thought I heard the words, "Jump if you like," in my head. Others heard it too because they got excited.

I watched in utter amazement and shear terror as some of the people on the bridge got up, climbed over the railing and jumped off the side as if they were bungy jumping or high diving. Each one of them fell out of my sight into the darkness, leaving only the echoes of their yells. Then, as I watched, each of them drifted up in a beam of blue colored light and disappeared into the night sky.

I was glad no one asked me to jump. I didn't want to even think about it. Soon my ears started to buzz and the blue light was surrounding me. I felt my body going up very quickly.

We were on the ship again. We walked to a small office like area to wait. It was only a few moments before Hetar came in and told us it was time for me to go home.

I didn't want to leave this man. He was so loving and gentle to me. I never wanted to go away from him. I told him I didn't want to go home without knowing his name. He told me, "Don't worry, you know my name. You just don't remember today." Then he smiled at me like I was some kind of cute child.

I was returned to my house on my feet. I removed the gown like dress they gave me, then put on my nightshirt, then sat on the bed. I watched as the little gray being walked into the wall and was gone.

Event 32
Subject: Paul
Date: 1992
Location: Canada

(Comment: Keep in mind, when you read this next event, Paul and Michelle had not met here on Earth. In fact, Michelle's first book "The Alien Abduction Survival Guide" had not been published yet and Paul had not spoken to anyone about his contact experiences. For the ease of telling, the name 'George' has been added to this account. When Paul first noted it, he did not clearly remember the name of the man involved, though he knew the name of woman he called Kris.

Note the sense of panic when Paul is told, George stopped working again. Paul is sure the reference is that George stopped making efforts for the good of the community in the particular role George was supposed to be filling.

Could it be that the aliens are not only training contactees to rebuild some kind of post-Earth-disaster community, but are also relying on their efforts to create this community, regardless of any individual abductee's level of remembrance?

Could this effort be so paramount, that when someone stops working, it creates panic in others?)

I had a very clear, very long experience. It was one of the most intense experiences I ever had to that date. The first thing I remembered was opening my eyes on shipboard. It was like I had just materialized on the ship or had just got sucked into it. When I opened my eyes, all my mental facilitates were immediately turned on and sharp. My memory was clear and I was confident. Everything was familiar and I knew exactly where I was. When I came back after the experience, I remembered not having as much knowledge about everything. It was as if part of my mind was switched on while there, then switched off again when I returned home to Earth.

I was standing in front of small gray alien. There were several other humans and aliens who were busy working at control panels in the room. The alien in front of me raised his left arm and telepathically projected the words to me, "Kris needs your help. George has stopped working." [Editors Note: Kris is the name the aliens often use when talking about Michelle]

I opened my eyes wide. I experienced a great sense of urgency and bolted out the door as fast as I could. As I ran, I turned around and yelled back, "Which way?"

"The way you are going," the alien responded telepathically. When he did, I knew exactly which way to go.

I ran as fast as I could down a series of hallways. I remember thinking that I had to be careful in case somebody mistook me for a runner. (A runner is someone who panics during an experience and runs trying to escape.) If they did, they might detain me. I did not have time to stop and explain. I tore through the halls passing some people and aliens along the way.

"Look out! A runner! Someone help!" I heard a woman shout. Then she tackled me on the left side of my body.

I was in a great hurry and I guess the woman was not very strong, because I was still able to move along, albeit clumsily, dragging her behind me. I reached over with my right hand to touch the woman so she would let me go. Then I heard a loud scream. She let go and I ran off.

"He's got a wand! Someone stop him!" a man shouted.

I stopped and turn around. There were several people standing around the woman who was lying on her stomach on the floor. All of them were looking at me.

One young man on the right leaned over to them and said quietly, "It's Andrew." [Editors Note: Andrew is the name the aliens often use when talking about Paul] He motioned with his hand, waving me off. He said, "Go. It's okay. Go."

I tried to catch my breath and walked over to them.

"Are you okay?" I asked the woman.

"Go, it's okay!" The man said again with force. "You're on your way to help someone aren't you?"

I remembered and whirled around, then ran off. I began to concentrate on making up the time I lost and something very strange happened. I began to literally fly down the halls at an amazing rate of speed. It was exhilarating and a bit scary. All the while I felt driven by this incredible sense of urgency to help Kris.

At one point, I flew past a whole bunch of people who were lined up against the walls of a hallway. They were staring blankly, like they were in some kind of trance.

I flew past an alien being who was standing watch in a hall. I heard his voice in my head say, "Andrew, slow down. You're going to hurt someone."

I slowed down to a physical run and came to a wide hall where there were more people. There was an alien standing in front of a small doorway on my left. He pointed to the door with and telepathically said, "She's up there."

I slowed down, turned into the door and leaped up the stairs. There was a group of people sitting in the room. A small gray alien was conducting a lecture. I recognized two people who were there and immediately went over and sat to one side of them. I realized that I should have sit between them, so I got up and did. On my right was George, and to my left was Kris. I put my arm around her.

I began to talk to George about something and became very involved with what I was saying. It began to get more and more difficult to talk with the lecture going on, so I suggested we go sit somewhere else. We walked out of the room, down the stairs and over to a room where there was a table and chairs. George sat across the table in front of me. Kris sat to my right.

I began to speak in earnest to George, telling him he had to keep working. George was unresponsive and kept telling me things like, "You don't know how hard it is, man!"

I tried to get him to be more communicative by being more sympathetic, granted my sympathy was not that sincere. I said to him things like, "I know it's hard and you took the hardest job of all." All the while I was thinking he had the easiest job of all of us.

"What happened to your beard?" Kris asked me.

I told her I shaved it off because of the way she reacted the last time she saw me with it. She didn't seem to fully recognize me, as though her memory of me had been partially removed and her consciousness had been pushed down the way the ET's sometimes will restrict our memory when they are trying to teach us something about ourselves.

George continued being unresponsive and argumentative. Every time I told him he had to keep working he would stand up and begin to swear and yell at me. I responded by telling him to calm down and that he did not have to yell. As soon as he calmed down, I started talking to him about his work again. In turn, he responded by becoming loud and crass with me.

An alien came over and touched George's hand. His eyes went blank and his limbs limp. He walked away peacefully with the alien.

Kris asked me where George was going and I told her he was going home now, but that we could go and talk some more. We walked for a bit and talked, then went over to one of the spots on the ship that transports people. Then we were on Earth.

We were standing on the outskirts of a small city or town. It was warm, even though it was very cold back home in Canada at the time. I remembered one of the street signs later when I returned. It was "El Peso".

As we walked, Kris asked me if we would be okay and I pointed up at the sky. There was a large, black triangle shaped craft hovering there. We walked along some streets, talking all the while until we got to a bridge that crossed in front of a huge dam.

"What is this place?" Kris asked me.

"This is our place. This is where it's going to happen," I replied.

There were several dozen people on the bridge. Some were dressed oddly, like they had just gotten out of bed. We walked along and talked. We came up to a group of people who we knew. They said something to Kris and I said to them, "Hey, give her a break. This is her time of purging."

We all spoke for a while about the problems Kris was having with George. We also talked about what life would be like after the 'change' happened. It was going to be a huge change and everything would be different for everyone.

After a bit, we walked down the bridge. We heard a voice tell us to get ready because it was time to leave. Kris and I both watched as a man stood up on the edge of the bridge, then jumped down into the vast darkness. I watched as he plunged several hundred feet down, then ducked my head quickly, not wishing to see the result.

I stood up a moment later and looked at Kris who stood watching. I followed her gaze and saw the man who had jumped off the bridge now floating up in a beam of blue light to the triangle above. Other people began to jump off the bridge.

Eventually a blue beam appeared around Kris and I. We flew up and into the ship through its hull.

We took Kris home and she was placed back into her house. I remember telling her how much I loved her and that I would always be there for her. It was hard to say goodbye to her, knowing she would have to deal with George the next day.

After Kris left, I went to a room that was similar to medical facility. I remember standing in front of the door thinking how good it was to see Kris and how good everything had gone. Then I took a deep breath and walked through the door that somehow opened automatically as I stepped into it. The woman I had knocked over earlier as I was running to get to Kris and George was inside. She was sitting on a table. There was a taller alien standing beside her. He looked at me and said to me telepathically, "Was that necessary?"

"I'm sorry. It was an emergency," I said.

"I hope so," the alien said. "Shouldn't you tell her you're sorry?" referring to the woman.

"That's what I came here for," I said. I looked over at the woman who appeared not to have heard the telepathic conversation that had just transpired. She looked at me as though wondering what was next.

"I'm very sorry," I said out loud. "Are you okay?"

She grabbed my arm by the wrist and said, "It's okay. I understand. You had to go help someone."

I put my hand on her neck. "I want to help you feel better," I said. I began to focus my energy. Her eyes widened and I could feel myself transmitting healing energy into her. I did this for about twenty seconds, then let go.

Section 2.3 Celebrities

In this section you will find accounts of people who believe they have met celebrities and public figures while in the company of the aliens. Often, these celebrities are in a position of attention, much as they would be during their earth-lives.

Abduction experiencers have reported almost every type and kind of celebrity. Actors, writers, artists and musicians are reported on a regular basis. Politicians are reported on a less frequent basis. Certain celebrities' names come up more often than others in reports. Because the celebrities in question have not come forward to tell the world they have had alien contact, we cannot say for sure that those perceived by abductees as being celebrities are, in actuality, the celebrities themselves.

With the aliens' power of illusion, it is possible that some of the celebrity sightings are screen visions created by the aliens.

Nevertheless, when you consider the frequency that some celebrities' names come up in reports from contactees, one has to wonder if those particular celebrities may be abductees themselves.

It is not a far reach to assume that if the aliens are trying to influence our society in any way, they would abduct public figures. Because of the popularity of some actors and musicians, it is conceivable that alien influence, via these people, would have more affect on the population at large, than if the aliens influenced politicians. Also, actors, writers, artists and musicians are far less likely to be bound by a political agenda and will follow their heart song when creating. If that heart song happens to be influenced by the aliens, then so will what they create.

In the following events, we name the celebrities who were reported. **We caution to tell you that we cannot and do not state that any of these celebrities were abducted and that the persons in these events are the actual celebrities.** Keep in mind the aliens' power of illusion.

(Editors note: The answer to your question is, NO. We have received very few reports of anyone seeing Elvis on a UFO, so we doubt that he's really up there with them.)

Event 33
Subject: Adult Female
Date: 1995
Location: United States

(Comment: In this event, the subject did not have a dialogue with the alleged celebrity, so there is no way of knowing if this was a representation of the celebrity or just someone who reminded the abductee of the person in question. We listed this event because it is very common that contactees will see people who remind them of certain celebrities and then assume they are, without any conversation to indicate they are right. Recognition in this manner is by far the most common type of report we received in this area.

Notice that the subject was asked to aid the man on the table. For some reason the subject did not react as one would expect. When she behaved inappropriately, she was made to leave.

Additional comment: This particular subject reported many events where she fought with the aliens, refused to do anything and became angered at humans around her. Likewise, she reported very little in the way community and pleasant interactions with the aliens.

One could easily jump to the conclusion that by fighting back, she was not subject to alien illusions of pleasant events, but this would be incorrect. The subject reported many events where illusion was effectively used on her.

It is more likely, that by fostering a belligerent attitude, she has been excluded from many of the pleasant events, or simply cannot remember them, as doing so would challenge her paradigm of "the evil aliens.")

The subject reported she was in the company of the gray aliens. She was brought into a room and saw someone who she believed was Charlie Sheen on a table.

She reported he was screaming and crying out in terror. She looked down at him. The gray being standing near her told her to calm him down. She found that seeing the man screaming was rather funny for some reason and almost bursts into laughter. Then, for a reason she did not understand, she started to yell at the man on the table, "You'll never be your father!"

Without warning, she found herself outside the room wondering if it was really Charlie Sheen and why she behaved that way.

Event 34
Subject: Paul
Date: 1998
Location: United States

(Comment: Paul, Michelle and another contactee all had recall of this event the morning after it occurred. The celebrity in this event was an active part of a group of people.)

I was standing in an alien base with a group of people. I looked to my side and standing next to me was someone who appeared to be the actor/comedian Robin Williams.

We were attending some kind of somber event, like a wake or a funeral. Williams was making a joke about the event in an attempt to lighten up the situation, but nobody seemed to appreciate the humor.

I wondered if it was the real Robin Williams or just someone who looked like him. I thought that maybe it was some kind illusion and it was really an alien pretending to be the man. Many in the room appeared to believe this person was Robin Williams. Whatever the case, the person darted around with gesticulations and tonal inflections that were exactly like Williams' voice and movements.

I woke up the next morning and said good morning to Michelle. The first thing she asked me was if I remembered attending some kind of funeral and that it was a very serious event.

"Did you see anyone strange there?" I asked.

Her eyes opened wide and she stared at me. "Yes," she answered, "actually I did. Believe it or not, I think it was Robin Williams."

I looked back with the same wide-eyed amazement. "Do you think it was really Robin Williams or someone making themselves look like him?"

"I don't know," she replied.

We both went on about our day. The next day on my return from work, Michelle informed me she had been speaking to a fellow contactee who lived on the west coast. She said that our friend also had a memory of being at a funeral that was attended by Robin Williams.

Event 35
Subject: Michelle
Date: 1996
Location: United States

(Comment: The celebrity subject of this encounter actually answered questions about the celebrity's work and played the part of the celebrity. Again, since this person has not made any public announcement that he is a contactee, we must assume there is a possibility that the celebrity was actually a screen vision.)

There were several of us in a room watching a small gray ET talk. When I walked out of this room, I seemed to be outside, but when I looked up I could see that the sky was not real. It was like a dome, high above the buildings. The sky seemed an unnaturally bright, white color. There were houses that looked like mobile homes all over the place. In the distance, there were mountains. There was little to see around me, except for some mobile homes and a few small buildings.

There were several women near a wooden building. They all appeared to be in their thirties. They were excited about something. I went over to see what the commotion was about. One of them told me that the singer/songwriter, Peter Gabriel was inside the building. I was wondered if he was really there or if it was some kind of screen vision. The doors opened and we all ran in to see.

There was a man sitting inside who looked very much like photos I have seen of Peter Gabriel. Someone asked him about his song writing and he was explaining that he took a lot of the inspiration for the strangest of his lyrics from these encounters. I looked away, through the open door and saw my contactee friend, Anne, outside. She seemed to be lost. I knew she was a big fan of Peter Gabriel's, so I ran out to the top of the steps that lead into the building and told her he was inside talking to people.

She was very excited about the idea of seeing him and began to run. She tripped and fell on the steps. Her shin was badly hurt, and she was in a lot of pain. Nevertheless, she managed to get inside and talk to the person who appeared to be Peter Gabriel. Later, before we parted, I heard her ask a gray alien if that was really Peter Gabriel or just some kind of mind trick. He told her to figure it out herself.

The next morning, I called my friend right away. The first thing I said was, "How is your shin?"

She was more than a little surprised that I knew about her shin. She explained that although it didn't make a lot of sense to her, she believed she was abducted the night before and brought to talk to Peter Gabriel, but on the way, she fell down. She said she woke with a painful and large bruise on her right shin.

Oddly enough, she didn't remember seeing me there at all.

Event 36
Subject: Adult Female
Date: 1994
Location: United States

(Comment: Many abductees believe that the music, art and entertainment they enjoy has hidden messages from alien sources in them. Could it be because the people creating these forms of entertainment are contactees, or is it simply that when someone feels as strongly about something, such as abductees feel about their experiences, it is easy to see your obsession in everything around you?)

The subject found herself sitting in a round, white room. She knew she was on an alien craft. She was confused at first, but then realized that she was not stunned and could move. She decided to walk down a curving hallway. She passed several rooms that had closed doors. She reported that she passed by a door and noticed it was opened.

She looked inside of the room and there was a small table with stool-like chairs around it. On the chair on the right was a small gray being. Another small gray being was standing in the room, near the table. On the left side she reported seeing a man who she thought looked very familiar. She described him as a short man with a pleasant smile and beautiful blue eyes.

He turned to her, and she asked him, "I know you, don't I?"

He nodded and said, "Listen to my music. It's all in there." As he said that, the small gray being who was standing, came over to the woman and took her by the hand and led her back to where she came from.

The next morning she rushed to a music store and searched until she found that man's face on a record cover. She then purchased many of the man's works. She reported being pleased with the music and believes there are messages in the music that are much like what she has learned in ET school. She reports having no doubt that the man on the ship and the man who makes the music are the same man.

Section 2.4 Spiritual Experiences

As in all societies, there has to be a thread of common belief to tie people together. In the alien community, that thread is often called *spirituality*.

We would first like to explain what we mean by spirituality, as the word has been used many times to mean many different things.

Unlike the spiritual movement of the late 19th century, the spirituality we are writing about does not revolve around crystal balls, seances and mystic mediums contacting the dead with ringing bells and horns.

When we speak of spirituality, we are talking about a non-religious concept which attempts to explain life and how it relates to both the physical and non-physical universe.

All physical, sentient beings — in this case human beings — face questions regarding the nature of their existence. Humans are limited by their physical boundaries and are required to take the existence of higher forces on faith. They most often do this by turning to organized religion. Unfortunately, for many experiencers, organized religion, with its dogmatic view of man being the pinnacle of God's creation, falls short.

Once contactees accept the reality of their experiences, the conflict between what they know is reality, versus what human based religion proclaims as truth, becomes irresolvable. This compels them to seek out alternatives to traditional belief systems. They search for one that fits the out-of-the-box model and their expanded view of the meaning of life.

Some speculate that the simple knowledge of alien existence creates this drive in experiencers to find a spiritual archetype beyond the traditional norm. Consider that this need may have already existed before the contactees themselves were ever aware of it.

Based on the encounters we have collected, it is clearly apparent that abductees already have an inherent sense of their spiritual connection to the universe. This connection is nurtured by their alien hosts.

In some, it may manifest as simply as a deep love of the Earth. In others, it can be such a strong driving force that it is the main focus of their day to day existence.

Whether an alien creation or the natural result of a peoples' need for answers, the spiritual side of the contact experience bonds people together regardless of cultural, social or religious backgrounds.

When choosing the following events we decided to bring you accounts that show examples of contactees exploring spiritual issues in the ET environment.

We do not go into explanations of exactly what any of these events could represent in a spiritual sense, nor do we explain spiritual issues from the viewpoint of the belief system of the contactees involved. We simply offer you these accounts of people interacting in the community in a spiritual sense.

Event 37
Subject: Child Female
Date: 1992
Location: Mexico

(Comment: Alien interactions with children are often more mild and supportive than those reported by adults. This could have many factors, the least of which is that children are not as likely to remember their events tainted with shades of fear?)

The subject, who is a child of ten years old, reported she was with an alien she called the head doctor. He told her he had a gift for her. He handed her a jar.

She opened the jar and said, "It's empty."

The gray alien said, "Look closely. The hand of God is inside."

She looked closer, but still didn't see anything.

The alien said, "Reach in there and see."

The subject was rather hesitant, but nevertheless, she reached inside. She felt around in the jar and said, "See. It is empty." She held the jar up, there was clearly nothing inside it, except her own hand.

The alien said, "No. The hand of God is inside. Don't you see it?"

Event 38
Subject: Teenage Female
Date: 1998
Location: United Kingdom

(Comment: Many abductees have reported finding themselves standing in a field, as described below. Almost all have reported seeing colored balls of light flying around them and/or UFOs overhead and feeling a strong sense of wonder or more.

Other contactees have reported seeing such balls of colored light in times of extreme stress, as if the lights were there to reassure the subject and help them through.)

The subject reported she was on an alien ship. She was on a table with a gray being staring at her. He told her to sit up and look at something he was holding in his hand. It was a bright ball of many colors of light. The subject reported she looked at it and got dizzy.

Next thing she was aware of, she was standing in the middle of a field. The grass was knee-high and there were people standing around her. In the distance, the subject saw mountains and hills.

She reported saw bright balls of light come out of the night sky and fly over the heads of the crowd. She wanted to reach up to touch one, but could not move.

The subject reported that the lights went away, leaving her standing there, overcome with a feeling of awe. She was then filled with a feeling that she described as, "Being one with God".

The subject reported the lights came back. This time they were attached to may UFO craft of different shapes. The subject said they flew around, as if dancing in the sky. She reported feeling wonderful. She said, "It is hard to explain, but I felt like God was inside me, in every part of my body. It felt very good."

Event 39
Subject: Adult Female
Date: 1997
Location: United States

(Comment: The subject of this event was experiencing terrible fear connected with her abductions. After this event, she reported that her sense of fear was greatly offset by the spiritual feels she now experiences during events.)

The subject reported she was lying in bed. She felt the sensation of floating. She could not open her eyes for some time. Once she was able to open her eyes, she found herself in the company of the gray aliens. A tall being that was standing next to her looked into her eyes and she was suddenly aware of the vastness of the universe.

She explained that this awareness was not just of the physical universe, but of more. She realized how vast creation was and how — despite the great size of creation and how small she was and how short her life would be in the timeline of eternity — she was important and she mattered.

The subject explained the experience changed her life. Before this event, she was depressed and felt like her life was pointless, despite her financial success. After this, she found new reasons for living and a spiritual life she never knew before.

She said that after this point, whenever she wakes from an abduction, even if she awakens with a feeling of fear or with unexplained marks, she always has a strong feeling of awe and of being fortunate that she is part of something special.

Event 40
Subject: Adult Male
Date: 1997
Location: Australia

(Comment: Often aliens will show a person something that will change their perspective about life and the Earth.

Many people have reported events like the one below. They almost always report an awe for what they observed, and pay little, if any, attention to the technology that got them there.)

The subject reported he was on a mountain top resting from his climb. He stood up and saw a bright circle of colored lights above him. Then, without warning, he was looking down at the mountain where he was just standing. Next he was looking down at the whole area for miles around where the mountain stood. Then he saw the surrounding cities.

He kept zooming away from the point where he stood, in like fashion, until he was looking down at the bright blue Earth from space. The subject said he looked on with amazement at the Earth, because it suddenly appeared to be very small in the sky. He was in awe of how small and fragile it looked.

The subject reported that as he looked at it, a voice said to him, "You know, this bubble of life in space is like a soap bubble in the air. A pin can pop it and it is gone."

The subject turned to the voice and saw it was a gray alien. He then got upset, thinking it was a threat from the alien directed at the Earth.

The subject said to the alien, "No. You don't pop that. That's where I live."

The alien said, "Yes. Don't ever let them do that." When he said that, the subject knew the alien was telling him that mankind could easily pop the bubble.

The subject said that just as the alien spoke, a beautiful glow came around from the side of the Earth and made it shine in a silver light. Then, as he watched, a bright white object that the subject believed was the Moon came from around the side of the Earth and shined light so bright he could no longer look in that direction.

The subject said that it was so breathtakingly beautiful, that he was overcome with a feeling of God and Creation. The subject reported that he was always searching for a spiritual connection to the Earth, but he never achieved it until that moment when he realized he was standing apart from the Earth, looking down at it.

Event 41
Subject: Adult Female
Date: 1994
Location: United States
(Comment: Subjects sometimes report seeing a person who provokes a strong spiritual reaction in them. Often, if the subject is from a Christian background they see a person the believe is Christ.

The following event is different. In the following event the subject was shown a strange animal that invoked such a reaction. Could this animal be a representation of an ancient god? If so, and if the intent of the aliens is to instill a sense of spiritual importance to an event, why show a contemporary woman with a strong Catholic upbringing a symbol so foreign to her religious background?)

The subject reported that she did not remember how she got there, but she found herself on what she knew was an alien ship. There were many gray aliens around her. She wasn't scared, but confused. One of the taller aliens came over to her and told her to be very quiet and not to move during a procedure. If she did, he would show her something amazing. She listened and tried very hard not to move. The subject did not recall what was done to her.

After it was over, the alien told her she had done well and he was going to show her something that was very special and extremely ancient. The being explained it came from the dawn of mankind and that few people ever witnessed anything like it.

The subject was intrigued and asked what it was.

The gray alien being replied, "A million-fingered monkey."

"Million-fingered monkey!" she said with surprised. "Why did you make a monkey with a million fingers?"

The gray said, "We did not make it. Although it is said to have a million fingers, it truly only has a few hundred fingers." He went on to explain to her that the million-fingered monkey was a powerful being from Earth's past.

The subject said she did not believe him.

The being then directed her to go into a small room and look for herself, which she did.

Inside, she found the monkey. She reported it was dull brown and about the size of a small dog. She reported it had the most bazaar hands she had ever seen. She said, "His hands branched out in what looked like the stems that are left when you eat a bunch of grapes. The fingers moved around like worms as the monkey moved. I was amazed and a bit shocked by the look of it."

The monkey sat up and faced the subject, starring right at her. She said she felt it could read her mind. She didn't know what to say or do.

The subject said, "When I looked at it, it was as if I was looking at some ancient God of some kind. There was a mystical feeling to the animal. I felt overcome with the feeling that it was somehow a spiritually higher being and it could see right into my soul."

The gray alien came into the room behind the subject and told her she had to go. She walked out with him and asked him if he had any other strange animals on shipboard. He said he did not, but there were others all over the place.

The subject said that since that day, the vision of the million-fingered monkey and how she felt in its presence stayed with her. She also said that she has no doubt it was exactly what the gray said it was — an ancient and powerful being from Earth's past.

Event 42
Subject: Adult Female
Date: 1997
Location: United States

(Comment: Sometimes a person's spiritual horizon is expanded by just knowing more exists. The next event was described as very powerful by the woman who experienced it, because it expanded her view of the Earth's spirit beyond the limits of our solar system.)

The subject, who is a Native American Elder, reported she was talking to a gray alien about the Earth as a living being. She told him how she believed that the Earth was alive and had a soul and a spirit. She asked the alien if his own world had such a soul and presence.

She asked the alien, "Does your world have a soul?"

The alien explained, "If a planet can have life on it, it must have life in it. It must have a soul to generate the spirits of those who live on it."

The subject asked, "If your spirit is generated from that planet, does your spirit get weak when you come to our planet?"

The alien replied, "The Earth adopts us when we are here. But since we are different from you, the energy of the Earth feels different to us."

The subject reported that the alien then asked her if she would share her feeling of the Earth with him. In exchange he would share his feeling of his world with her. She agreed.

The subject said the gray alien floated into the air to face here, then put his forehead to hers. She looked deep into his eyes and began to see something. The subject reported that she envisioned herself standing on the alien's world. She saw it as he remembered it. She believed he was seeing Earth through her eyes as well.

The place she saw had two suns in the sky, nevertheless, it was dimly lit. She said it was much like twilight here on Earth. She was warm and there were many trees there. She said she could feel the presence of the alien's planet under her feet.

The energy she felt did not feel the same as Earth at all, yet the feeling around her was not so alien that she felt totally disassociated from the place. She said she knew then that the Great Spirit was truly everywhere and that planets each had their own souls.

Event 43
Subject: Adult Male
Date: 1994
Location: United Kingdom

(Comment: Events suggest that the gray aliens often leave the teaching of spiritual issues to other alien beings.

Though not always, in general, the stronger a subject believes in spiritual issues, the more events they will have of the following nature. Yet this is not always the case.

Many abductees who are far more conventional in their views of religion — or have no view at all — experience these types of events. Some question if people who are looking for a "new spiritual view" of life create their events to reflect their beliefs. We have found it is just the opposite. A person will often create their human spiritual understanding based on what they have experienced in the company of the aliens.)

The subject reported he was abducted by aliens and brought onto shipboard. He was informed by an alien that he was to attend a class. He was brought to a room that was completely circular. The ceiling was very high, and the walls were smooth. When he walked in, the door closed behind him and gave him the impression of being in a carnival ride that spins around, pressing all the riders to the wall.

After a while, the door opened again, and a man — who the subject reported as being not quiet human — came in and sat down. He said to the subject, "I must tell you about the Kabala."

The subject replied, "The Kabala. I know of the Kabala. Of course I know of the Kabala."

The teacher demanded of the subject, "Tell me what you know of the Kabala."

The subject said he went on to tell the man all he knew about the tree of life. Suddenly, as the subject spoke, the teacher pointed to the floor and a tree grew right in the middle of the room. The subject described the tree as follows: "It grew in the center of the room. At the end of each limb of the tree were these lights. And the lights were God."

The subject went on to say that he was overcome with a sense of awe that he could not describe. He said, "Suddenly all the rhetoric, and all the labels of what these branches meant...was nonsense. All of a sudden, it was so simple. There were no words needed. Just to see those lights and to know that they were God was absolutely breathtaking. It made sense, looking at the tree of life, and seeing how it reached into the universe. It was no longer a just a concept. It was a connection to eternity."

Event 44
Subject: Adult Male
Date: 1990
Location: United Kingdom

(Comment: In the next event, the focus of the encounter appears to be to show the subject that there is more to spirituality than the tools one can use. The alien reinforces that the subject's own efforts are important, not any tool, talisman or object they own.

Why are these beings making such an effort to correct a subject's misled faith in objects? If the aliens had no true concern as to how a person preformed the tasks put before them, why would it matter? If the man could do what they wanted him to do and still believe in the power of his rocks, why make the effort to change this, unless there is true concern with the subject's spiritual well being?)

The subject reported he had been searching from teacher to teacher, guru to guru, looking for answers. He claimed he read every book he could and did everything to try reach his spiritual height. Nevertheless, his results were far from what he expected for his efforts.

One day, he was at home meditating using some crystals and a human-like alien woman, who was very tall, appeared in the room. He reported with emphasis that she was physically there. She was not a vision or dream.

The alien woman looked at the crystals he was holding and said, "They are very pretty, aren't they?"

He replied, "Yes. This one is for tuning your spirit. This one opens up your heart chakra. This one heals the body..."

She replied, "Oh, I see." She took them into her hand and asked. "What do you think will happen if I do this?" Then she tossed the rocks across the floor of his parlor. They sparkled in the sunlight that was coming in from the windows.

He said, "I don't know."

She said, "Aren't they pretty?"

He said, "Yes." He was confused as to why she tossed them on the floor to begin with.

She asked, "Are they helping your spirit tune, or your heart chakra now?"

"I don't know. Maybe," the subject said. "I don't think they work on the floor," he continued. He reported that he reached down to pick them up. When he did, the being projected the telepathic thought to him that the stones were not important.

He turned to her and said, "I need these. They are tools to help open my soul. How am I ever going to become? I want to be awake. I need my rocks. I need every tool I can get. I want to be like..." be began to name off many spiritual teachers he idolized.

The alien said, "You are like them. You are identical. But what is more important is that you are also unique."

He looked at her and protested that he still needed the tools to get somewhere with his spiritual quest.

She looked down at the rocks one more time and once again said, "They are very pretty, aren't they?" Then she looked at him and said, "Your tools are much more beautiful. Your tools are in your eyes. Look in your eyes."

The subject then walked to a mirror and looked into his own eyes. Then he experienced a vision of being drawn into his own eyes. He saw himself standing in a place that looked very much like a desert, with large sculpted rock hills. When he turned the alien woman was there.

She said, "Do you see those rocks?" She pointed to the incredibly beautiful rock cliffs that towered around them. The subject said he nodded. "They are very pretty, aren't they?" she said once again. "Are they not much more beautiful than the simple stones you think you need so badly. Yet this is your soul." She held out the small crystals that had been on the floor in his home, and then pointed to the complex, and magnificent, shinning rock walls around them and said, "Which tools do you think are greater? Which do you depend on?"

The subject reported he then said something to the effect of, "But I just want to be awake."

The alien woman replied, "You will never be awake so long as you put your energy and faith into rocks, before you put it into your own soul."

The subject said it was difficult to portray in words the feelings and emotions connected with what she said, but it changed his life.

Event 45
Subject: Adult Female
Date: 1998
Location: Mexico

(Comment: The next three events illustrate a lesser-known fact. Many contactees participate in elaborately structured ceremonies that appear to commemorate everything from rights of passage to celebrations.

Of all the events the media and some researchers ignore — because they do not fit into the accepted medical template — memories of ceremonies tend to be disregarded as fabrication regardless of the number who report very similar events.

Could this be because the idea of a non-earth-based, organized, spiritual community represents a direct threat to the traditional dogma of existing belief systems and the politically powerful religions that fuel them?

All three events come from people in different countries, proving the global nature of the spiritual theme of the phenomena, which is not restricted to any geographical region or cultural background.

In the first event the subject participates as the initiate. Take note of the surroundings. Many ceremonies reported by contactees take place in a magically lit, cave-like setting).

The subject reported being brought to a cave of shimmering, shinning rocks. She was dressed in a long white dress. There was a water fountain in the middle of the cave that gave off a glowing light. There were beings made of light standing around her that were very beautiful to look at. She also reported seeing several smaller gray aliens in the room.

The beings of light asked her questions, such as: Was she willing to speak the truth even when the truth was not what others wanted to hear? Was she willing to always look for light, even when darkness surrounded her? Was she willing to open her ears to the sounds of life around her?

After answering the questions, the light beings surrounded her. She then bent down and put her face into the water from the fountain and washed it over her hair. When she stood up, the setting had changed. She was no longer in the cave, but was now in a large room with walls that looked to be cut from quarts or crystal. There was an intense buzzing in her ears and she remembered nothing more.

Event 46
Subject: Michelle
Date: 1998
Location: United States

(Comment: In this event, Michelle is preparing to take part in a ceremony. Once again the ceremony is to take place in a magical, cave-like setting.)

I was led into a room by several small, gray beings. They combed my hair and helped me to put on a long white and purple dress. After I was ready, they brought me into a small ship. I did not feel it moving, but knew it was taking me some place.

When we arrived, I exited the ship to find myself on a beach. It was either very early morning, or very late evening. The circle of the sun was just over the water. I did not stand on the beach long enough to notice if it was rising or setting.

I walked from the beach into a large, natural cave in a rock outcropping, not far from where we stopped. Once inside, I touched some symbols on the wall and seemed to be drawn right through the wall into a vast opening on the other side.

The opened area was beautiful. It was lit with what seemed like candlelight that twinkled around the cave, but it had no apparent source. In the center of the cave was a very beautiful water fountain. I wanted to run to the fountain to take a closer look, but I knew that was not appropriate behavior. I was there to oversee some kind of initiation and had to behave in a serious, somber manner.

I went into a small side room that was brightly lit. It had a comfortable sofa-like piece of furniture in it. Another woman greeted me there. We discussed the "new girl" — the initiate who we were going to indoctrinate. I remember hearing what sounded like hundreds of children singing and I knew it was time to get started. I straightened out my dress and checked my hair, then headed for the door. The cave was now more brightly lit with twinkling lights. It was beautiful to see.

I saw the woman who was the subject of the ceremony entering the hall. She was accompanied by four small gray beings and two taller grays. The other woman and I greeted her and the ceremony began.

The ceremony, like most, consisted of a lot of talking. In this case about truth and spiritual growth. After the ceremony ended I was led back outside and into the transport ship which looked more or less like a cube with rounded corners.

Event 47
Subject: Adult Male
Date: 1997
Location: United Kingdom

(Comment: In this event, the subject recalls, with vivid detail, the particulars of a teacher initiation ceremony. The subject said such recall was possible because he performed this ceremony countless times through his life.

Considering this, plus the two previous events, it is clear that these unrelated people in different parts of the world, and from different cultures and religious backgrounds — as well as many others whose events we used in our research — are experiencing the exact same thing.

The implications of this are impacting, as it suggests a spiritual, hierarchically structured community, which is maintained in the alien environment.

As vehicles such as the Internet help to recreate the alien based contactee community here on Earth, will this spiritual, hierarchical structure follow?)

The subject reported he was dressed in a brilliant purple and white robe. It had gold trim. He was presiding over some kind of ceremony. He knew at the time exactly what it was and what he was doing. He said he was not nervous or afraid and felt like he had done this many times before.

The subject described the setting as a large cave-like place, or an underground grotto. The wall behind him was lined with seating similar to that of an auditorium. In the middle of the room was a large fountain. Water ran out of the fountain and into a channel on the ground that led to a pool by the side of the room.

The subject was standing by the pool. He described it as being five feet across and ten feet long. He observed a ramp that led into the pool, then back out again. The water in the pool was gently swirling. From where he stood he could see beyond the pool. There was a door to the right that was hidden from everyone else's view by a wall.

There were many alien beings there. The subject reported seeing several human-like ETs, who were more than seven feet tall, standing by the chairs. There were also at least a dozen gray beings present. They seemed to all be watching from the audience.

As the subject stood facing the pool, to his left was an area where there were three large, ornate chairs and two tall, torch-like lights on golden sticks. The light from the torches gave the place a magical and mystical feeling.

Someone announced the beginning of the ceremony and then a man dressed in white and gold, accompanied by three other adults, walked out of the door and came into view of the audience. He announced, "I have taught these children. They have learned well. It is time for them to take their place among those who teach."

The subject asked, "Who are these children?" He reported it was as if he were following a script.

The other man replied, "The first is named William. He has earned the right to teach."

The subject reported that William walked forward. He was wearing a dark colored robe. He dropped his robe and walked into the water and submerged up to his armpits, then lowered himself so his head was under. He came back up, then walked toward the subject.

When William emerged from the water, two humans who where standing by the pool put a light blue robe on him. Then the subject turned to face him.

The subject asked, "Are you ready to take your place?"

William replied, "Yes, I am."

The subject touched William's ears with his hands and said, "I open your ears that they may always hear the truth when it is spoken to you. That you may hear the messages in the wind and know the wisdom of silence."

Then the subject put his hands on William's face with his thumbs over the other man's eyes and said, "I open your eyes that you may see the truth when it is before you. May you always see the good that is in all things."

Then the subject slid his thumbs down and opened the William's mouth with them, and said, "I open your mouth that you may speak the truth. That your words will not be wasted on lies or vanity."

Then the subject put his right hand on William's forehead and his left hand on William's chest, and said, "I open your mind that you may know the truth from all the chaos that appears to be truth. And so you will have the wisdom to listen, speak and teach the truth. And I open your heart that you will have the courage to do all these things when your heart tells you it is time."

The subject reported he then pulled William's head forward and kissed the man on the forehead and said, "You are now a teacher. The truth is your power. Be strong. Be happy."

William replied, "My strength and joy come from the truth."

At that point the subject reported that he moved out of the way and William walked past him. William took a seat in one of the large chairs.

The subject reported doing the same thing with two more people, using the same exact dialogue. He reported remembering that one was a man named Robert and the other a woman named Lori. After they were seated in their chairs, his part of the ceremony was over. The subject remembered giving them some kind of quick speech about responsibility, which he could not recall in total. He left the ceremonial area through another door that was hidden from the audience's view.

Event 48
Subject: Adult Male
Date: 1997
Location: Australia

(Comment: Could the following event truly be an example of aliens joining in a human ceremony here on Earth? The tribal people of this subject consider their relationship with the gray beings to be almost that of family. They are not surprised that their extended family would appear for such an event.

The fact that the aliens would take the time and effort to be present at such an event indicates that these events are of importance to them.)

The subject, who is an aborigine from Australia reported he was walking to a holy place of his people. He was required to make a quest there for a sacred ceremony. When he got to the holy place, he started his ceremony. He was standing in the center of a large rock formation, praying.

The subject said he looked up and saw a bright light. He saw five beams of light come down around him and he reported the beams turned into beings of light. The subject described them as being made of light, but physical nonetheless.

He reported that soon after, six gray beings appeared as well. He said that he was not surprised, because his people believe that if you are truly blessed, these beings will come to you during the particular ceremony he was performing. He said his people do not see them as aliens. They see them as a type of extended family. He had no doubt whatsoever that the beings were there to take part in the ceremony with him.

He said that many of his people have seen them and feel close to them, though it is not something they usually tell outsiders.

Chapter 3
Bases and Places

One of the biggest questions people ask when it comes to UFOs and aliens are, where are they? Not just in the sky, but where are they based?

Many contactees have theories and opinions as to where these places are, based on their experiences. Yet no one can tell you the exact location of these bases, here or Earth or otherwise.

What they can tell you, without a shadow of a doubt, is that these bases do exist and are frequented by both aliens and humans alike.

In the following chapter we will examine events that happened on alien created or occupied bases and cities, as well as experiences where the display of technology seems to be the focus of the event.

It may not come as a surprise to most people that the alien visitors to planet Earth have set up housekeeping here. It may not even surprise you that many experiencers believe they have visited alien run bases on other planets such as the Moon and Mars. It will probably surprise you that many contactees reported being with the aliens in places that could only be described as a human made city. A few abductees (who do not know each other) even came up with the name of this city. Of the few that did, all but one called it "Omega City."

When you read the following chapters, remember that all these events could fall into other sections of this book. We placed them here because of their strong descriptions of the setting.

When you read these accounts, be ever mindful that these are not dreams. These are actual events people recalled consciously. Although many abductees do report reoccurring dreams of such places and things, the stories included were not taken from any source that described the event as a dream.

Section 3.1 Toilet Turmoil

Where are the alien bases? How big are they? What do they look like? Are they hidden under infamous *Area 51*? Are they the source of the mysterious *Taos hum*? Are they sucking up the government's *black-ops* budget?

The answers to the above questions are anyone's guess. Abductees have opinions, but from what we have seen, abductees truly don't know any more about the answers to those questions than anyone else. What abductees do know is the answer to these questions: Do alien bases exist? What do they look like inside? And what goes on in these bases?

Personally, we believe the answers to those questions are far more interesting than if there is a metallic object sitting at the bottom of Groom Lake.

There are some questions you may never dare to ask about alien bases, but abductees have to face all the time. For example, where are the bathrooms and how do they work?

Ask just about any abductee with memories of being in an alien base for any length of time and you are bound to find what we call "bathroom stories".

It would seem that the aliens don't have much concern for housekeeping, as humans understand it. This could be because — based on information given by several contactees we spoke to — the aliens do not have to worry about cleaning up after themselves. Their ships are self-cleaning in some way as are their bases. But, are all the bathroom on bases built by aliens?

If what contactees remember is correct, it would appear that somewhere on this Earth — perhaps in several places — there are locations that seem to be human built, with cement block walls, tiled linoleum floors and wooden doors.

These human-like areas have been built onto by the aliens, so there are areas where the bases are obviously not human built and other parts that are.

It is easy to wonder, considering the alien schoolrooms, if these parts of the buildings were created by the aliens to look like old human buildings. This is possible, but in our opinion, not as likely, because of the "bathroom stories".

As you read the following events, pay attention to the bathroom stories and ask yourself, does it sound like these areas were created to be like this? If so, what benefit do the aliens get from this type of situation? Finally, would it make more sense if these bases were, in fact, former human facilities that the aliens did not maintain?

If you opt for the latter, then you have to ask, who gave them such places?

Once again, it is only right that we remind you, with the aliens ability to create illusion, these toilet turmoil tests could be some strange form of reaction tests.

The bathroom stories are not pretty, but due to the shear number we received, it is clear they are something people remember.

Event 49
Subject: Adult Female
Date: 1997
Location: United States
(Comment: This event is extremely typical. Most people who remember bathrooms on base tell almost this exact same story.)

The subject reported she was on an alien base that she believed was underground. She reported she is often taken there. The subject said the place appeared to be made by humans. She described the base as being very human looking, but also very run down. She said that it was clammy and damp, without windows. She also reported it had linoleum tiles on the floor that were uneven. In a different part of the base it was the way she remembered alien ships to be like — with smooth, curving, white walls.

The subject reported she had to go to the bathroom badly. She did not want to go because she knew, from previous experiences, that the bathrooms in that part of the building were terribly dirty. Still, she could not wait any longer and went to look for a bathroom.

The following is the subjects account of what she found:

"I entered the bathroom and the stalls were painted with a gray paint. They were scratched up. The smell was indescribably horrid. I opened the first door, and the toilet was filled to the rim with waste. It was obvious it was clogged up, and had been for a long time. The door to the second stall was missing. The toilet was in the same condition — full. I opened the third door to find the toilet was missing altogether. Finally, it was too much for me to hold it any longer. I found a toilet that was disgustingly dirty, but at least not filled to the rim. I used it, being careful not to let it touch my body. "

Event 50
Subject: Adult Male
Date: 1999
Location: United Kingdom

(Comment: Could this be a test of some kind? If so, what would be gained by causing a person to soil themselves on a dirty fixture? Could it simply be that aliens are poor housekeepers, and when nature calls, it can be overwhelming?)

The subject reported this is just one of several experiences involving dirty bathrooms on an alien base.

The subject was with a group of people looking for a bathroom they could use. The area they were in appeared to be quite old and the walls were made of concrete. Several doors to different rooms lined the hallways. They walked through a number of long hallways before they finally found a bathroom.The subject reported it was filthy.

Inside the bathroom were a number of stalls and urinals. Most of the people he was with chose to suffer rather than use the facilities. The subject reported that he could not wait, so he hunkered down and used one anyway. When he was done, the people looked at him and remarked at what a ghastly mess he was from contact with the toilet.

A few moments later a gray ET walked in. He was familiar to the subject.

"Look what you've done to yourself!" the alien said to him telepathically.

"I really had to go bad. I was desperate," the subject tried to explain.

"Come. We have to cleaned you up," the alien said.

The subject reported that he was embarrassed, but physically relieved. The back of his legs felt uncomfortable and messy. When he returned home, there was no evidence of his ordeal.

Event 51
Subject: Paul
Date: 1998
Location: United States

(Comment: Paul could not remember what would make a man jump into a filthy urinal, probably because he didn't think it was a good reason.

It should be pointed out, regardless of the fact that many believe having bathroom related dreams signify a cleansing of the soul, these types of events do not appear to have any spiritual significance. They appear to only be physical events that happened while in the alien environment. Perhaps, because of their nature, they are simply easier to recall for most people.)

I was standing in a large men's bathroom that contained a number of urinals. Each urinal ran from the floor to about chest height. Water was running down the urinals almost continuously. They were dirty, but they served their purpose. There were many men in the room relieving themselves.

Suddenly a man ran in and tossed his whole body in one of the urinals so that the flushing water poured over his head. The image stuck clear in my mind as water ran over his bald head. He looked like he was about to faint. All of us looked him and were somewhat repulsed by what he had done. To jump into a urinal was bad enough. To jump into such a dirty one was even worse.

I stood for a moment talking to some other people who I knew. A minute later I left. After a few moments, the man who had thrown himself in the urinal appeared and was standing on my left. He began talking to me. He seemed quite lucid and began explaining to me why he had thrown himself into the flushing urinal. Still, it didn't make much sense to me.

I looked ahead to find that I was standing in a line of people who were all walking down a hallway. In front of us were some gray aliens. They were filing everyone from the line into a doorway down the hall.

Everyone moved quite matter-of-factly, as though they knew exactly what they were doing and where they were going. Soon I saw my wife, Michelle, in the line. I went up to her and we walked together. As we did, I told her about what happened in the bathroom.

She said, "Don't use the old bathrooms. Use their bathrooms. They have a different symbol over them like this." Then motioned with her hands to create a specific symbol she knew was above the doorways of the ET bathrooms.

Event 52
Subject: Paul
Date: 1998
Location: United States
(Comment: Some have speculated that the aliens don't even consume food or produce waist, and this is why they care little for clean bathrooms. If this were so, then why are there alien bathrooms and why are they so clean?)

I remembered what my wife said about using the aliens' bathrooms rather than the dirty human ones, next time I was picked up by the ETs.

That night, I found myself on shipboard. I was in a totally white room. It was very bright and very clean. I was sitting on some kind of hospital-type of bed in an open area divided by white curtains.

On my right, stood a gray ET holding a device in his hand. It looked like a small, hand-held, soldering gun but it had no sharp tip on the end.

"Ready?" he asked.

"Okay, go," I said.

He placed the device against my arm. He pressed a trigger like device and I felt a pressure on my arms that increased in stages. Each time there was a blast of pressure, it felt like something went deeper into my arm. On the top of the device I could see a red L.E.D.-like readout that changed its display with each blast. After the fourth blast, he stopped.

"Okay, done," he said. He reached down and gently pulled my legs up to help me lay down on the bed. I felt immediately dizzy and woozy. The sensation felt similar to getting a demorral shot.

As I started to settle a bit, I realized I had to urinate. "Darn, I have to go to the bathroom. I should have done that before," I thought to myself.

About twelve feet in front of me was a door with the symbol on it that Michelle had described before. Inside the room, I found a strange type of toilet. The toilet looked to be made of a porcelain-like material. It was bright white, with a saddle shaped bowl. It appeared that the proper way to use it would be to straddle it. The bathroom around the toilet was very, very clean and everything looked newly washed and polished.

I don't know how the toilet flushed after I left, but I assumed there was some kind of flushing action.

Event 53
Subject: Adult Male
Date: 1999
Location: United Kingdom

(Comment: Many abductees have reported strange rashes and fungal infections on odd parts of their bodies over the years. Could the following experience explain where these rashes are coming from?

Swimming in a pool during an abduction is not as uncommon an experience as you may think.)

The subject reported he was in the company of the gray aliens. He was someplace that he believed was underground. It looked like it was human made. It was dirty, in disrepair and the roof was leaking in places.

The subject had to go to the bathroom very badly. He began to search for a washroom. He found several places labeled "men's room." In each, he reported the smell was horrible. The toilets were missing, or filled to the brim with waste and debris. The urinals were broken and smashed.

He walked through that area in hope of finding a clean bathroom. He found a very large men's room. But once again it was completely disgusting and destroyed. He walked through the room, and found some shower stalls at the back. They, too, were dirty. There were no lights in this part of the room. The subject noticed light coming from a door in front of him. He headed for the light and passed into a room with long corridors of metal lockers on both sides. He passed through this room, and into the next. It opened up to an area where there was an Olympic sized, in-ground pool.

The subject reported that the water in the pool was disgustingly dirty, green, and overgrown with algae. The smell from the pool rivaled the smell from the dirty bathrooms. He also said that there were humans playing in the pool. They seemed to be having a wonderful time. They appeared to be totally unaware of the revolting state the pool was in. There were several gray aliens standing around as if they were life guards.

He said he was shocked. The smell was overpowering and he hurried back the way he came.

This same subject mentioned that later that same year, he was once again in the same place. This time he was sitting on a table. A light was being beamed over him. Where it touched him, it tingled.

After the procedure was over, the alien standing by him said he could join his friends and go for a swim. The subject reported thinking it was a great idea.

Some other humans that the subject knew in the ET environment, but did not have any memory of ever meeting under normal circumstances, joined him and they were led through the same area he walked through on his own before.

This time, the rooms appeared to him as spotlessly clean and in perfect condition. Everything was sparkling and beautiful. There was no foul smell.

When they entered the room where the pool was, the subject recalled a distinct smell of chlorine, like one would expect around a swimming pool. There was no hint of the foul, algae scent he smelled before.

The subject reported that he and the others eagerly jumped into the swimming pool.

After a few moments, he found himself thinking that something was not right. He recalled the last time he was in the area and found himself struggling to know which reality was the truth. The more he questioned, the more he started to see things as they were. First he realized the water, that appeared crystal clear and clean, felt thick and murky to the touch. He also realized that the pristine, blue painted, concrete bottom of the pool felt soft, mushy and slimy between his toes.

He reported that it then occurred to him that despite the fact he was seeing a beautiful crystal clear pool, he was actually standing waist deep in the swampy pool he recalled from the previous experience.

He reported that he started to get out of the water, and a lifeguard came walking over to him and asked him why he was getting out. He said although the lifeguard looked like a human, the subject believed he must have been a gray alien. The lifeguard suggested he go back into the pool and enjoy himself. When he refused, the lifeguard told him he would have to be hosed off after swimming, and directed him to an area on the pool patio where the lifeguard rinsed the man off.

The next morning the subject woke up with a rash all over his backside.

Section 3.2 Moon Malls?

We have heard many accounts from abductees who are positive, without a shadow of a doubt, they have been on alien bases located on the Moon. What they report seeing there is surprising to say the least. A good number of extremely credible people have come forward — albeit reluctantly in some cases — to report what they saw there.

The most common and consistent of these odd accounts concerns a three level mall, complete with stores, escalators and shoppers.

Historically, these accounts are disregard as fabrications or dreams. After all, why would an alien race bother to build a human mall (or a replica of a human mall) on the Moon? What could they possibly gain from such an effort?

You may be tempted to assume that such a place was built as some kind of testing ground where human subjects are put through their paces. Yet, if this were so, then one would expect to receive reports of people experiencing odd events in these malls. To the contrary, almost all the events we heard were mundane accounts of walking or window shopping in the mall.

Nevertheless, can we continue to ignore these accounts as dreams or flights of the unstable just because we are flabbergasted by their content?

If it were one event, maybe we could. If even two accounts matched, you would have to think about it, but you could put it off. What about more than thirty?

Event 54
Subject: Adult Male
Date: 1997
Location: United Kingdom

(Comment: The following is representative of the majority of the accounts we received from people who claimed to be on a base on the Moon. Most people are extremely hesitant to talk about what they know is up there because of how unlikely it is. Odd though it seems, both authors have seen it first hand, too. Is it on the Moon? Who knows for sure. We were told it was, as were many other people.)

The subject reported being told by gray aliens that he was on a base they built inside the moon. He was hesitant to talk about this memory, because it seemed to be so strange that even he wasn't sure he believed what he saw on the base.

He described the base as being almost all underground. In places the sky looked like a painted surface that was not very high over the ground. In other places it seemed to be clear and open, so one could see the stars above. In yet other places, the ceiling seemed to be glowing with daylight that did not appear to be coming from any one spot, much in the same way Earth's sunlight is defused on a cloudy day.

While on the *moonbase*, the aliens showed the subject areas where they built small human-like neighborhoods with things such as houses, apartment buildings, and even what appeared to be a trailer park. He also reported that inside the base there was what appeared to be a three-level, human, shopping mall, complete with escalators and shopping crowds.

He reported that some of the stores appeared to be offering very human products, such as shoes and cosmetics, etc. Other stores displayed items in their windows that the subject did not find recognizable at all.

The subject reported seeing what looked like fields, hills and cities under painted skies on the moonbase.

Event 55
Subject: Adult Female
Date: 1996
Location: United States

(Comment: Although this event is here because of its setting, it could easily be put in several other categories. Take note of how the alien's suggestion of future events may have actually created them.)

The subject reported that the gray aliens often take her to a place she believes is built inside the moon. She reported that it looks like a human city. She said there are houses, stores, animals and even a mall there.

The subject said that the aliens often bring her to an apartment in a small, multi-leveled building. She described the apartment as her "home on the base". The woman reported she has several friends who also frequent the same base. They are brought together on a regular basis so they may interact with each other much in the same way as any other neighbors would.

The subject relayed an event where she was at this apartment, when someone knocked on her door. She opened the door to find a gray alien standing in the hall. She let him in and he told her that she was going to become pregnant. With his words, he telepathically transmitted to her the concept of her being pregnant in the true human sense of the word, for a full nine months. She found that quiet surprising, because she had no intention of having any

117

more children. She asked him how and why. He told her it was nothing to worry about and asked her to follow him. She wasn't sure if she wanted to, but she did anyway.

She followed him down the hall and through a panel in the wall that seemed to dissolve when they touched it. On the other side of the wall, was a medical like facility. She was led to a table and asked to lie down, which she did.

A taller gray being touched her face and she saw nothing else. She felt a strong pressure on her abdomen. When she could see again, she asked the gray why they made her pregnant. He explained that he didn't, and that she and her husband were soon to conceive a child. When she did, the implant he just put inside of her would aid in the growth and birth of the child that would otherwise not make it.

The woman was confused and concerned. When she was returned home, she remembered the procedure and wondered if it were true that she and her husband would soon be having another child. Her own children were in their teens and she was not planning anymore.

The more she thought about having a new baby, the more she began to think it was not a bad idea. She told her husband about the event and of being told they would soon have another child. To her surprise, her husband seemed to totally disregard the element of alien intervention, and thought having a new baby was a fantastic idea. Not long after, the woman conceived and now has another child.

Section 3.3 Omega City

Is there really a whole town somewhere on Earth set aside for alien use? Could Omega City be one such town? The accounts of contactees who have clear memories of being brought to a city by their alien hosts indicates that there is such a place.

Where is it? Some have said it is in the southern United States, others have said, with the same conviction, that it is on the Moon. But everyone agrees it really exists. Descriptions of this city are strikingly similar, not just from abductee to abductee, but also from event to event. People describe being taken to the same place again and again. Some claim to have homes and apartments there. Many can draw road maps. If Omega City is truly here on Earth, then it means the aliens are right under our noses.

The following events take place in Omega City. They were selected because the subject actually used the name "Omega City" in their account. There are other events in other sections of this book which take place in what appears to be an alien created city. Those events likely happened in Omega City as well, as the descriptions were similar, yet they are not included here because the name was not included in the report.

Event 56
Subject: Adult Female
Date: 1999
Location: United States
(Comment: Just as with the previous accounts, the events could fall into other sections of this book, but they were put in this area because of the emphasis on the setting.)

The subject reported being taken by the aliens to a place she called "Omega City." She reported having clear memories of buildings that seemed to be human made, as well as buildings that appeared to be only fronts of buildings for show — like one would see on a movie set. She said some of the buildings were normal inside, albeit rather run down. Some were obviously not made by any conventional, human building method inside. She described the latter building interiors as having rounded, white walls and a "plastic-like" appearance.

She explained that the downtown area is the only part of the town that where you can find real buildings. She reported along with several shop-like buildings, there is a carnival, a city hall and not far from the center of town, what she believed is a drive-in theater.

She reported having many encounters in this place over the years. When asked where the city is, she was not sure. Nevertheless, the subject had no doubt it was a real place that is either totally created, or built onto by the aliens.

Several other contactees have described such a place in our interviews. Another person we interviewed who had no knowledge of, or contact with this subject, reported a name for this place as well. She, too, called it Omega City.

Event 57
Subject: Adult Female
Date: 1997
Location: United States

(Comment: The subject of this account also used the name Omega City when recalling the following event. She reported this was a conscious event, although she admits she has many dreams or dream-like events that happen in the same setting.)

The subject reported being taken by aliens to the place she knows as Omega City. She was told to go through the city and find a particular man. As she searched, she came across a long line of people walking single file down a road. The people seemed very upset. She asked what was going on. Someone explained to her that the city had been destroyed and they were leaving it to find a safe place. The people were very somber and quiet as they shuffled down the road.

She assumed that the person she was sent to find could be in this line, so she started to question everyone in the line, asking if they were this man or if they knew where she could find him. The more she talked to these people, the more she began to loose herself in the illusion they were under. She began to believe that she, too, was part of a group of people fleeing a destroyed city.

She kept looking back at Omega City and could see that it was not destroyed. But her mind still believed it was. She began to repeat to herself, "I know this isn't real." Soon she forgot she was involved in an alien encounter at all and truly believed she was one of a group of refugees leaving a destroyed city in search of a safe place.

Eventually, she and the group came to a chain-link fence. Beyond it was a yard that dropped down to a paved lot. Behind the lot was a large brick mill. She was compelled to leave the line and walk down to the mill. When she got there, a man opened the door. She described the man as, "Claiming to be human, but he looked like a puppet of a human."

The man asked her to come into the building, which she did. He questioned her about the group she was with. The subject reported that she told him she was running away from the aliens. She said she needed to get her head clear from their influence so she would know what was going on again.

The man then told her that there was no such thing as aliens. She insisted there were. The subject reported the man kept leading her in a conversation of looped logic, trying to convince her that there were no aliens and that she only needed some rest.

The subject reported that after short time, she became very tired and was convinced to put her head down for a moment and rest. Which she did. When she awoke she was in her own bed.

Event 58
Subject: Adult Woman
Date: 1996
Location: United States

(Comment: Does this event prove not only prove the existence of Omega City, but that it is run, at least in part, by some human government or organization? Could this be another ET illusion?

The woman who recalled this event was so afraid of the implications, that she refused to acknowledge it as real, for a long time. It wasn't until another abductee mentioned to her the name Omega City that she realized something had to be said.)

The subject reported she woke in her bedroom and believed she was being abducted by aliens, only to open her eyes to find herself sitting in a room with three human men. They were dressed in neutral colored suits. They were showing her a film of what appeared to be a 1950's newsreel. It was black and white and there was no sound.

As the subject watched, one man explained what she was looking at. This is what the subject reported: "In the first scene of the movie, there was a shot of a desert-like area with low rolling hills in the distance. Over the hills came a round silver-white object. It flew quickly and didn't leave any vapor trail. It stopped over an open area of a yard that was surrounded by a tall fence. There were several, one story, very plain looking buildings behind the craft. There were no symbols or writing on the craft. It landed on several long legs.

"The next scene is of five human men; most of them dressed in dress shirts. One had on a tie. Two had their sleeves rolled up. None of them were wearing dress coats or suit coats. It appeared to be very hot out. They were standing by the craft. There was a ramp out of the craft just as if it were from an old science fiction movie."

The subject went on to describe how several gray beings came out of the craft and shook hands with the humans. As they did, one of the men showing the film told the subject the name of each man in the reception line. The only name she recalled was "Follie". She said that the man showing the film told her that Mr. Follie's presence dated the film because he was struck dead of a heart attack just three months after the film was made.

The subject reported that the aliens looked like very typical gray beings. There were three tall ones and two shorter ones. They give one of the humans a small white box. The movie had no sound so she could not hear if anything was said.

The movie scene changed. The new scene showed a military jeep-like vehicle on a flat paved area in the desert. The subject believed it was a runway. The alien craft hovered motionlessly next to the Earth vehicle. The screen split so that under the picture of the craft and jeep was a display of the jeep's speedometer and some other analogue dials.

The movie showed a man standing between the two vehicles wave a flag and the jeep took off at full speed. The craft followed.

The dials under the screen were pinned to the right, indicating the Earth vehicle was at maximum speed. The jeep passed an orange traffic cone on the road, then slammed on its breaks. It skidded to a stop. The UFO craft stopped exactly over the cone, apparently without slowing at all.

The movie scene changed again to that of the UFO craft making acrobatic passes through the frame of view over and over again. It stopped without slowing and took off at great velocity from a dead stop. It hovered and turned in the sky. The subject watched for a while in amazement, then the movie ended.

The men explained to her that now that she has seen the film, she would have to witness the fact that it was being shown in compliance with some treaty. The subject agreed and the men led her to a large black limousine.

She got into the car and it drove down a long road behind what she believed to be an airport. As they went further down the road, she started to believe it was not a regular airport because she reported seeing a very tall, barbed wire, topped fence with lookout stations along its length.

The subject reported the road on which they rode became more and more bumpy. She looked out of the window at the sides of the road. They became more over grown with plants and trees as they drove further. She reported seeing a few old bordered up houses or sheds on the side of the road.

The subject said that after some time, they turned onto even smaller roads in worse condition. Eventually they stopped.

The subject reported that she was amazed to see the area was lit with floodlights. There were two other limousines parked there already when the subject's car arrived. The people in the other cars got out.

The subject reported there were more suited men and two other men who were dressed in street clothes. One of those men was very thin and about thirty years old. He wore glasses. The other man was about sixty. He was overweight and seemed to be glad to be there.

The subject said she turned her attention to an area behind where they parked. It was an old drive-in movie theater. The ticket kiosk still stood. There were letters on it that were, at some points, broken and hanging. They spelled out "Omega 8 Drive-in Theater."

The 8 was hanging funny, and the subject said it could have been the infinity symbol. She wasn't sure.

In the drive-in parking lot, all the rows of speakers were still standing, though they were not in good condition. The projection booth was still there and it was showing a movie on the screen.

The subject was sure it was the same movie she was just shown in the office area. She reported the whole drive-in was covered with some kind of mesh of ropes and hanging fabrics that she assumed to be form of camouflage.

The man who came with her from the office explained that, as in agreement with the treaty with the aliens, the movie was being shown. As agreed, it was being shown in public and in an open area since its release decades ago. He explained to the subject that in order to fulfill the part of the agreement that stated it must received a certain number of human viewings, it was being shown twenty-four hours a day, seven days a week, three hundred and sixty-five days a year to their man in the projection booth. It was exactly by the letter of the contract, he said.

The subject reported she told the man, "It might be by the letter and thus legal. But if you bend all the words around you can make it fit with the agreement, but it's not morally correct," she said. She told the man, "You're just playing word games."

The subject reported the man replied, "That's the nature of treaties. If they didn't like word games, they should've been more precise."

The subject said the man asked her and the other two guests if what was happening fit the exact wording of the treaty. The large man said, "Yes. Most definitely." The younger man and the subject were hesitant. They then were returned to their respective limousines and left.

Upon entering the vehicle, the subject reported that the man next to her grabbed her arm and she suddenly felt very dizzy. She blacked out. She didn't come to until late the next morning. She awoke on the sofa even though she went to bed in her room the night before.

Section 3.4 Technology

In the following events people describe seeing extraterrestrial craft operating up close while in the alien environment.

It is not uncommon for abduction experiencers to have UFO sightings here on Earth. The majority of those we have spoken with over the years have had some kind of craft sighting on Earth.

Abductee reports of craft they see during contact experiences are usually closer, in greater detailed and more impacting than those reported by others. Yet, since these sightings happen in the context of an abduction experience, they are usually never considered when examining the phenomena of alien craft and alien craft behavior.

Although technology commonly reported in the media is limited to such things as medical instruments, there are other things people remember.

Event 59
Subject: Paul
Date: 1999
Location: United States

(Comment: Sometimes contactees are treated to shows of technology without any apparent reason. Are the aliens showing off? Are they giving the contactee a reward of some kind? Was the contactee simply in the right place at the right time?

Some people who see craft close up report an emotional and spiritual reaction beyond a sense of awe.)

During an contact event, I found myself standing on a gently rolling hillside on a warm, breezy, starlit night. I was surrounded by a dozen or so people. I could feel the wind as it blew along the hair on my forearms. Above us hovered a massive ship, unlike anything I had ever seen before. For all intents and purposes it looked like an upside down wedding cake. It appeared to be about ten stories in height and was made up of gold panels that glowed, emitting a brilliant light. It looked like a small, inverted city. There was no sound coming from the craft at all.

All of a sudden, the huge craft flew in an arc over a hill so that it was completely out of sight. Less than two seconds later, I saw the craft shoot straight up at a tremendous rate of speed.

I heard someone say, "Wow."

The craft traveled until it was just a small dot in the heavens, like a star. Then it shot sideways across the sky and disappeared. It was amazing to watch the craft flying above us.

I was overcome with an exhilarating, emotional reaction from seeing the craft.

Event 60
Subject: Adult Male
Date: 1996
Location: Australia

(Comment: In this event, we see alien technology used to test someone's ability to predict a future event. Even though this event comes from Australia, we have received several reports of a similar room with colored lights from different parts of the globe.

What purpose would it serve the aliens to teach humans this type of skill? After all, aliens have already demonstrated an ability to see the future, thus would not need humans to do it for them.)

The subject reported he was walking in the wilderness. He stopped to rest. He reported seeing a strange, white "thing" in the sky. At first he thought it was a cloud, which was strange because it was not the season for clouds.

As he watched it, he reported that it came down to the ground. The subject was confused because he was sure it was a cloud. Then he saw gray aliens coming out of it and he knew it wasn't a cloud. Though he reported it still clearly appeared to be a cloud.

They asked him if he wanted to go for a ride with them and he agreed.

Once inside, the subject reported the aliens made him take off all his clothes and they checked his body. The subject said they looked through his hair. He wondered if they were looking for lice.

They gave him his clothes back, and brought him to a room that was dark. The subject reported that little lights were flashing around the room randomly. The aliens had the subject point to each light as it lit and tell them what color it was. He was made to do it faster and faster, until he was telling them where the light would be and what color it would be before it appeared.

Event 61
Subject: Adult Female
Date: 1997
Location: Mexico

(Comment: Is this another case of being in the right place at the right time?)

The subject reported she was taken by the gray aliens to a large field of waving grass. The sky was dark, with just a hint of a glowing light coming over distant hills.

There were about twenty other people standing there as well. Among them were her husband and children.

She turned and watched the glow coming from the hill get brighter until it became obvious to her that it was coming from an object rising from behind the hill.

The object crested over the top of the hill and began to spin. It gave off a rainbow of colors as it spun, bathing the subject and her family in beams of colored light.

After a few moments, it glowed brighter and brighter. It soon stopped, leaving only a smooth, round, gray object in the sky. The object did not make a sound. After a few more seconds, it shot off into the sky and was gone.

Event 62
Subject: Adult Female
Date: 1989
Location: United States

(Comment: You may have heard of the term, "front door amnesia". It is used to describe how some people will suddenly loose recall of an abduction event the moment they enter an alien craft, only to have their memory start up again upon exiting the craft.

Due to this phenomenon, it is common for researchers to get reports from subjects who recall walking to and from ships, but not what happens while they are on the ships.

The following event came from someone who suffered from front door amnesia. Nevertheless, what they do recall is fascinating.)

The subject reported she was woken up by a strong buzzing in her ear. When she opened her eyes she found that she was floating out of her room, and through the wall. She was brought to land on her feet outside of a large, round object.

The subject believed it was white, but reported it looked gray in the moonlight. It was hovering, totally still and silently, about three feet over the ground on what the subject described as "a cushion of light".

She walked up to the object and asked the being standing by her side if she could touch it. The being told her she could, so long as she did not put her body in the light below it.

She agreed, then walked up to the object and stroked its smooth cool surface.

The subject said she was surprised how cool the object was. She expected it to feel hot. She also said the metal seemed soft to the touch, yet it was not yielding at all.

When the subject touched the vehicle, she reported the hair on the back of her neck stood on end and she was covered with "goose bumps".

The gray being then asked her to follow him into the ship. She reported that she was nervous about following him and asked if she could go back into the house and get her husband. The gray alien refused. She reluctantly followed him into the ship. Her memory stopped at that point, only to pick up when she was walking toward her home.

Event 63
Subject: Adult Male
Date: 1999
Location: Australia
(Comment: If the alien's have musical instruments, one can assume they have an appreciation of music. If aliens are

actually emotionless, robotic beings, why would they have a need to create musical instruments and make music?

A love of music implies emotional need and love of beauty. These are attributes that are seldom attached to the aliens by researchers and the media.)

The subject reported that the gray aliens talked to him about his love of music, then told him they had musical instruments as well. He asked to see one. The alien brought him to a panel. It had short beams of colored light coming off of it.

The subject reported that when he waved his hand across the beams they made a tone. When he moved his hand to lengthen or shorten any particular beam, it did not change the quality of the tone, but it did change the scale in which the tone was played, making it a higher or lower sound of the same note.

The subject said he was having great fun playing it. He reported that he could not find anything on Earth that made a comparable sound until he heard a glass harmonica played in a museum.

Event 64
Subject: Adult Female
Date: 1996
Location: United States

(Comment: Could it be technology rather than psychic ability that creates screen illusions? This next event suggests that the aliens' illusions could be created by the room the subject is in.)

The subject reported that in the middle of a contact event she became aware that she was very hungry. She told the tall gray who she worked with. He led her to room to get something to eat. The room was bare with the exception of a platter that sat on a table. A lid covered the platter. The subject asked what was under the lid.

The gray told her it was human meat and she was free to eat as much as she wanted. He removed the lid from the platter and left.

The subject believed he meant meat from a human body. The subject said she felt sick at the thought of it. She felt even more sick, because the smell of the meat was alluring. Nevertheless, she did not touch it.

After a while, the tall gray came back in. He asked her why she did not eat anything, since she was hungry.

She told him that she would not eat another human. It was not the right thing to do. She explained that maybe some humans have eaten human meat to survive or because it was their culture to be cannibals, but she was not like that. Then she demanded to know where he got the human meat in the first place.

He looked surprised. He told her it was not really meat at all. It was only an illusion. The being then pointed behind her to the table where the meat was.

She turned to look. What once looked like meat, now looked like something the subject described as bright yellow tofu.

She touched the tofu-like substance. It had the consistency of pudding.

The alien assured her that it was not human meat, that it was a protein paste substance. He told her there was technology in the room that allowed her to envision the protein paste to have any look or taste she preferred. He explained that the room could make the paste look and taste like anything her mind could imagine it to be.

The gray explained that he did not know the subject would believe his pun about human meat and create that vision for the paste.

She reported that she believed he was probably telling her the truth, but she decided to pass on the food.

Event 65
Subject: Adult Female
Date: 1997
Location: United States

(Comment: Three people described the following place. None of the three subjects knew each other. Several more reported places that seemed similar to this place. Could it really exist?)

The subject reported that she was on an alien craft. She was looking out a window toward a small building in the middle of nowhere. It was surrounded by a tall fence and barbed wire. All around it, was only desert and sparse, low shrubs. She did not recall seeing a road to the place.

The craft landed and she walked through a tunnel-like exit into the building. Once inside, she was led to an elevator by a taller gray alien being. She reported the elevator buttons did not have numbers on the, only symbols. She also said that the elevator must have gone down because the building was small and only one story tall.

She begged the alien being if she could see "them" again.

He was reluctant at first, but then gave into her request. He stopped the elevator by pressing one of the buttons. The doors opened to a long hallway that the subject described as being lit in much the same way as art gallery.

She and the alien stepped out of the elevator and walked down the hall together.

Along both sides of the hall were openings to display rooms. Inside each room was a different kind of UFO, or alien craft.

She looked at them with awe. After their tour was over, they returned to the elevator and continued down to a level where it opened up into an area that looked human made. They walked through this area and into an area that looked like the interior of the ship she arrived in.

Chapter 4
Visions

Much of the abduction experience revolves around visions. As we explored earlier, the aliens use visions to help contactees experience and practice events before they happen. They also appear to use visions to reinforce ideas and to explain spiritual concepts. Visions are also useful tools the aliens employ to ensure their safety and to help their human contacts deal with the shock of seeing them.

These types of visions are commonly called screen visions. Almost all abductees will experience screen visions of one form or another throughout their lives. Nevertheless, by far, the most common alien induced visions reported by contactees involve the end of the world.

Is the world in danger of encountering a series of cataclysmic events so severe that life on Earth will be totally changed? Aliens have been telling abductees this for many years now, through the use of visions.

The nature of the visions varies widely. Subjects have reported seeing everything from comets impacting the planet, to a massive flashover from a nuclear war that strips the Earth of its atmosphere. Regardless of the method, the result is the same; the event renders our home desolate of life.

Many people are of the opinion that the use of visions is to create terror in humans for some sinister, underlying motive only the ETs are aware of. If this is the reason, why are subjects forced to experience the same vision over and over again, even beyond the point of desensitization so they no longer feel terror? Especially when one considers the fact that the aliens could so easily remove any memory, thus keeping the fear factor fresh in the subject's mind.

Could these visions be tools for somehow helping or educating the subject? There is an obvious benefit to placing an individual in a situation or role, thus forcing them to deal with it in a controlled environment. In the case of recurring visions, the subject has the opportunity to acclimatize and work through a particular situation or peril. Their responses can be observed and suggestions can be given to help them deal with the event should it actually arise.

Many subjects reported developing a very different view of the Earth and their relationship to the Earth after experiencing the apocalyptic visions provided by the aliens. The realization of how fragile our home planet is, brings most contactees a new appreciation for this bubble of life in space.

Just about all the experiencers we contacted indicated a strong personal belief that the Earth and humanity are headed toward a massive physical and psychic change unparalleled in all of human history.

When looking at any ET provided visions, whether they are screens, apocalyptic visions or otherwise, we need to consider why the vision was used, what factors cause the vision to take the exact form it does, and who is the ultimate benefactor of the results. These are the clues that may help us better understand, not only the purpose of the visions, but the motives of the beings who create them.

Section 4.1 Screen Memories

To some, the idea of waking up to find an owl sitting on the end of your bed talking to you, or looking out your window to find a fully lit Christmas Tree standing in your backyard in July, sounds like madness. To contactees, it may not seem strange at all. Of all the tools aliens use, screen memories are the most easy to spot. That is, of course, unless you are currently experiencing one.

It is impossible to know how many screen memories abductees will experience in their lifetime. But it is a good bet the number would be staggering. This is because screen memories are used by the aliens for many different reasons and at many different times.

Most often, screen memories are used to hide an abduction event all together. For example, someone who was planning on visiting the beach may be abducted, and be kept with the aliens for the duration of the day. When they are returned, they will have complete memory of their day at the beach. They may never be the wiser if no one missed them that day.

Other times, screen memories are used to hide the aliens or their craft, so as not to scare someone they are contacting.

Of course, other times screen memories are used to create the illusion of a situation so a person can be trained or their reaction to something can be measured. (See Chapter 1, Section 2. Reaction Tests)

Screen memories have also been used to entertain and on occasion, to help the aliens take part in the human experience.

As you read the following accounts, consider the reason the aliens may have induced a screen memory. One may be quick to jump to the conclusion that they are doing it to protect themselves and hide from their subjects. Yet we believe, if you look deeper, you may find yourself looking at the screen memory phenomena from an angle of compassion on the alien's part for the human subjects.

Screen memories can and do break. Sometimes they can be broken during the event. If the subject touches something that does not fit what he is seeing, or if he is strong in his conviction that he is involved in a screen event, he may be able to break out of it. Other times, screen events can undo themselves with time, meditation, or hypnosis.

Sometimes, after a screen event, a contactee can simply look at the memory and — if it is bizarre enough — reason that it must have been a screen, and the illusion often dissolves.

Event 66
Subject: Adult Female
Date: 1995
Location: United States

(Comment: The woman who reported this event has a long history of contact with the aliens. On several occasions, she has seen craft close up, yet this time the aliens decided to use a screen memory to block her ability to see their craft.

Could the reason for this be that only her daughter was the subject of the contact this time, as the woman had no memory of contact herself that evening?)

The subject reported waking at about 3 a.m. with the feeling that someone was in her house. She opened her eyes and saw a strange light coming from her backyard. She didn't have any lights in the backyard. Although her home bordered on a neighborhood baseball park, the floodlights in the park were turned off at 10 p.m. every night.

She got out of her bed and went to her window. Outside, in her yard, she reported seeing what looked exactly like a large house, all decorated in tiny, colored, Christmas lights, sitting in the middle of the ball field.

She thought for a moment about how odd it was, since it was July. She looked at it for a moment, thinking about how beautiful it was. The longer she looked, the more excited she became. She decided to wake her husband and daughter so they could see the beautiful house.

She ran into her daughters room to wake the child. To her surprise, the child — who was seven years old — was sitting up in bed. The child said to her mother that she just had a dream that the aliens had come to visit again. The subject then realized that the object she saw in the back of her house was an alien craft.

Seeing that her daughter was not upset and seemed to be in fine health, she ran back to the other side of the house to look into the backyard again. This time, there was no trace of the Christmas lights, house or any craft. All she saw was the dark, empty baseball field.

Event 67
Subject: Child Male
Date: 1968
Location: United Kingdom

(Comment: Often, screen memories are used in the manner described below. Though the following involves a child, many times adults experience virtually the same events.

The fact that the aliens use screen illusions in order not to frighten contactees is more likely to be for the benefit of the contactee than the aliens.

With the aliens' technology and ability to paralyze humans, there is no need for them to go through any charades in order to protect themselves from contactees.

Considering this, it makes no sense that they would go through such elaborate charades to avoid creating fear in a subject if they did not care about the emotional state of the subject.)

When the subject was about six years old, he woke up to find an owl sitting on his bed. For some reason the owl had long legs, but it did not seem odd to the subject at the time.

The owl said, "I have a magic place I want to take you."

The subject asked if his brother could come with them. The owl said no. The owl instructed the child to climb on his back and suddenly he was flying. They got to the owl's home, where "doctor owls" came over and gave the subject a medical examination. The subject remembers the examination as being very much like a typical doctor's examination, except they looked at his bottom as well.

When the doctor owls were done, the first owl talked to him about school work and about his family. The owl told him that someday he was going to do important things and make people happy.

After that, the owl flew him home, put him in bed, then told him not to make a sound. The owl flew out the window and was gone.

Event 68
Subject: Michelle
Date: 1967
Location: United States
(Comment: Screen memories are not always animals.)

I woke up from sleep because I thought I heard a voice. I was wide awake and thinking about going to the kitchen to get a glass of water, when I saw something move by the wall. My bedroom had a slanted ceiling and the small dresser I had by the wall made a hollow cubby space between the dresser and the wall. I noticed something sitting inside that space. It was crouched down with its legs folded up so that its knees were at its chin.

I looked at it for a while and wondered how it got there. I could only image it was a large doll. I was sitting up in bed, staring at it when it moved. I jumped back in surprise.

The doll, that appeared to be dressed in the tight fitting outfit of a medieval harlequin dancer, walked over to my bed.

The doll touched my arm and told me with its thoughts to come with it. We walked toward the window. Before we took more than two steps, a bright, blue light came through the window and I found myself looking at my feet and then the ground far below.

I was taken to a large, oval shaped room. There were benches built into the walls. They were formed from the wall and were smooth and flat. There were many children in the room and in the center of the room stood a gray alien.

It appeared to me that he was dancing. I started to cry. I didn't want to be there because I had recently told my mother and father about my experiences and they told me that I was having nightmares. I was confused and frightened.

I was pretty much ignored as I sat on the bench and cried. I looked up from my tears at the alien in the center of the room, but once again I only saw a dancing harlequin doll.

Each child in the room, in turn, went into the center of the room and danced with the harlequin doll. When it was my turn, the doll called me to the center to dance with him. He was not demanding or mean, but I was afraid because I was sure I was having a nightmare like my parents explained.

I told him I wanted to go home. I cried. He drew me to him and I floated into the center of the room. He held out his hand and showed me a beautiful ball of purple light. Just then, I felt very loved. It was as if he were trying to comfort me. Nevertheless, I screamed at him that my mother said he was a nightmare and a boogie man!

He thought to me, "You are my child. I love you."

I started to cry again, "No I'm not. I'm my mommy's child! Not the boogie man's child!"

He seemed sad and I felt awkward that I made him feel sad. He said to me, "You can go home if that will make you happy."

I said, "Yes."

He told me to go with the monkey behind me and it would take me home.

I turned around to find a very friendly looking chimpanzee standing behind me. I took the monkey's hand and it brought me to a room with a big gray circle on the floor. He told me to stand on the circle. He stood next to me.

I realized then that chimpanzees couldn't talk and when he stepped onto the circle, as if to confirm my fear, he no longer appeared to be a chimp, but was now an alien.

I started to cry and tried to run. He grabbed my arm. His fingers wrapped all the way around my little child's arm. He held me tightly.

The next thing knew, I was lying in my bed and the alien who once looked like a chimp was floating backwards out the window.

Event 69
Subject: Child Female (as relayed by mother)
Date: 1987
Location: United States

(Comment: Accounts of screen memories from children are the most intriguing because they do not try and break the screen illusion. They ride the illusion, powered by their imagination. The accounts they give have a detail that most adults would miss, simply because they would not be able to fit it into their paradigm.)

The subject was a girl who was seven years old and in second grade. The subject's mother said her child knew nothing of the mother's abduction events. One morning, the child came running into the mother's room all ablaze with words about a very strange thing that just happened to her. She was visibly excited and a bit agitated.

The child explained that she was woken up as she lay in bed the night before by very short knights in silver armor. The child said the knights had big, bug-like helmets on and they were all silver and gray. She said that they asked her if she wanted to go play with them in their castle that was in the sky.

The child agreed and they took her by the hand. She said she was suddenly inside their castle. The child described the inside of the castle as being very strange, with little for furniture. She also said it was full of people who didn't have all their clothes on, as well as lots of the little silver knights.

One of the knights told her that she was sick and had to see the doctor. She didn't want to go, but he told her she had to go.

She said she cried, but they took her to the doctor's room anyway. In the doctor's room, the doctor held what she described as a colored flashlight on her. It made her whole body feel tingly. She said they showed her a panel of buttons and told her to push the buttons in the same sequence that they pushed them, like they were playing a game. They added more and more buttons until she could not do it without making mistakes, then they stopped.

The child said that later they showed a picture of a bird that she had to watch. While she watched it, she had to make it go up and down and side to side without touching it. She added that it was really hard to do and she didn't like doing it.

When her mother asked her how she got back from the castle, the child said the knights brought her home on a flying wagon and then told her they would come back before her birthday, which was almost a full year away.

Event 70
Subject: Michelle
Date: 1972
Location: United States

(Comment: The following event was one of my fondest memories from childhood. It was an afternoon I knew I would always remember. I was to find out that it was an afternoon that never happened.

When I first broke this screen memory and realized the truth, I was sad that I had lost such a special event. Later, I became angry that I was lied to. Then I realized that what seemed like a lie to me, was actually an act of compassion of the part of the aliens'.

Had I not worked to break the illusion, I would to this day still believe this very special afternoon happened, as my cousins and brother probably still believe.)

It was the summer. My family and I were camping. My uncle and aunt and their children came to visit. All of the kids went off to have fun in the woods. We were walking down a trail we knew led to a natural clearing in the woods where my brother and I had set up our own "club". As we walked, my cousin Lee said she saw something moving in the bushes and she didn't want to go any further. She was the youngest in the group and we figured she was just being a baby.

When we got closer to the clearing, we saw a pony standing in the path. It was a beautiful horse. It was all golden brown with a brown main. My cousin Mike, who was the oldest, said, "Let's be very quiet and maybe we can pat it." So we quietly sneaked up on the horse.

As we got closer, the animal retreated into the woods. We started to chase it. We made it into the clearing to find the horse standing there along with four other horses. We started to pat them and talk to them. We were all amazed that the horses were just standing there.

I decided to try and ride one of them. So I chose a beautiful roan pony and climbed onto its back with amazing ease. My brother and cousins did the same with the other horses.

We rode the horses around the field for some time. We had the most wonderful afternoon, shouting and playing and racing as we rode these friendly animals, bare-back and without bridles or reins.

After a while, we all felt like it was time to go. We dismounted the animals and walked back to the campsite. We were all sore and achy, which I attributed to the running and riding.

When we got back to our campsite, we told our parents about the horses. They didn't believe us. So my grandfather decided to take a walk with us to the glade to see where the animals were. When we got there, there were no horses, not even one hoof print in the dirt. He scolded us for lying.

We believed it and we were undaunted. For many summers we would recall the horses we found in the woods. For some reason though, by the time we were all in high school, the whole event seemed like a dream and we never spoke about it anymore. If anyone mentioned it, we believed it was just a fantasy we shared.

Many years later, when I was working in a meditative state, I was trying hard to see an event from my childhood that I had only partial memory of and the entire afternoon came back to me. Suddenly the whole vision changed in my mind. I saw — very clearly — that there was no horse standing in the path. It was a small gray being. He ran off and we followed him. When we got to the clearing, there were four other gray beings there. They each came over to us, one on one, and led us into a round craft that was hovering just above the ground.

I remembered asking, "What are we doing?"

The gray replied, "What do you want to do?"

My cousin Lee said, "I want to ride a pretty horse."

The gray responded, "That is what you will do then."

We were brought onto the ship and separated into different rooms. The inside of the ship seemed so much bigger than the outside. I don't know what they did to my cousins, but they gave me some kind of check up. Then they ran a beam of a blue-green light over my body. They moved my legs in a funny way, as if they were peddling a bike for me with my legs, then they told me it was time for me to go home.

When I was brought outside, my cousin Lee and my brother were there. We had to wait a few moments for Mike to come out of the ship.

One of the taller grays said, "You have just had the most wonderful afternoon. You found wild horses and they loved you and gave you rides. You played and were happy. Now it's time for you to go home."

We all nodded and walked away, not knowing it never happened.

Event 71
Subject: Adult Male
Date: 1999
Location: United Kingdom

(Comment: The following event is a good example of how the aliens will sometimes use screen visions to get a person to talk to them or open up about issues.

As you read this, take particular notice of how easy it was for this subject, a well off, professional man in his early fifties, to be taken in by the illusion.)

The subject had been watching a television show on Abraham Lincoln and had him on his mind when we went to bed. During the night, he was woken up by his cat. He couldn't get back to sleep, so he decided to go use the bathroom, but he never made it to the bathroom. He blacked out to find himself someplace else.

He reported he was sitting on a bench in a "strangely rounded room." Moments later, a gray alien came into the room and approached him. The subject told the alien to go away and refused to talk to him. Without a struggle, the gray left.

A few minutes later, someone who appeared to be Abraham Lincoln walked into the room. He was wearing a tall hat and black suit. He looked like one would expect Abraham Lincoln to look if he just walked out of a history book. Lincoln walked in and quietly sat down next to the subject.

Although he knew it did not make sense, the subject pondered if the figure sitting next to him was really Lincoln. He began to wonder if the aliens had a way of reviving the dead. He lost himself in the moment and found himself believing the person sitting beside him was, in fact, the real Abraham Lincoln.

The subject reported speaking to Lincoln for what seemed like ten or more minutes about things he heard on the television show. Lincoln spoke to him about the behavior of mankind and the structure of society. The subject did not find this strange at all. He felt that it was exactly the type of conversation he would have expected to have with Abraham Lincoln. He described the conversation as "fascinating".

After the conversation was over, Lincoln reached over as if to embrace the subject. The subject was taken by surprised and pulled back before he could be hugged. He stood up to shake Lincoln's hand. Lincoln stood up as well.

At this point, the subject reported feeling awkward that he did not accept the gesture from this American Icon. So, he reached out and gave the figure, who appeared to be Abraham Lincoln, a hug. When he did, he was surprised to find that there was nothing there to hug.

He put his hands down, and in the process, he touched something. He then realized that even though he was looking at a man who appeared to be better than six feet tall, he was touching a figure that was just about the sized of a child. Suddenly, he knew that it was a gray being, probably the same one that approached him earlier.

Event 72
Subject: Paul
Date: 1999
Location: United States

(Comment: In the next event, the screen memory is used to create a setting. Because of the use of the screen, no one in the event was scared or traumatized in any way.

So, though it can be argued that screen memories are used as a tool to manipulate people, thus making it easier for the aliens to control them, it can also be argued that it is better for the humans involved when screen memories are used to lessen fearful situations and create a sense of calm.)

I felt the ETs in the room and became very dizzy. I started to regain my steadiness to find myself standing in a large, old warehouse. At first I thought I was on one of the larger ships, but I soon discovered I was on a base held by the ET's.

I was talking to some gray aliens that were standing in front of me. We finished our conversation and a huge door in front of them closed. I turned to my left and walked over to an area where there was an old merry-go-round. It was broken down and dilapidated.

As I looked at it, an area of it seemed to transform. Directly in front of me, the merry-go-round suddenly appeared restored and seemed like it was brand new. I looked to my left and right and could see that it was an illusion. Outside of a six-foot range of vision, the merry-go-round was still broken and dilapidated. Nevertheless, in a six-foot area in front of me, it appeared beautiful and pristine. It also appeared to be moving! I could here sounds of a carnival. Then I saw small gray aliens bring children onto the merry-go-round.

The children believed they were riding on the beautiful, new merry-go-round. In that six-foot area of space, it all seemed to be real and in motion. The colors were beautiful and alive.

My wife, Michelle, walked up from behind me and stood just in front of me. She was looking at the amusement park ride, too. Others soon joined us. A small crowd was forming. Then, little grays entered the area. The appeared to be dressed up like clowns. They walked through the crowd putting some type of noisy vibrator on each person's left hand. They held it there for a period of about a minute each. I could see that within the illusion the ETs were creating, the people thought that it was some type of hilarious device that was a part of the carnival entertainment. People laughed when it was done to them, and they seem so be anxious for their turns. No one appeared to be in any pain.

One of the little gray beings came up to me with the device in his hand. He motioned, indicating that it was my turn. I said, "Oh no, I couldn't. It would freak me out too much. You do it to them."

He kept insisting. I kept cordially refusing. All the while, as this happened, I could feel my left hand buzzing. Oddly enough, I did not want to look down at my hand. After about a minute, the little gray alien walked away. I didn't realize at the time what the buzzing feeling on my hand was. I figured out later that they had performed the procedure on me anyway. It was not unpleasant, but felt rather odd.

Everybody was laughing and having a tremendously fun time. At some point everything went black for me and the next thing I remembered was sitting up in my bed. I got up to go to the bathroom and when I came back Michelle was sitting up in bed, wide-awake.

"We just got back," she said.

"What did you think of the carnival?" I asked.

"It really was a merry-go-round," she said with mild surprise.

"Yes, but it was broken. They only made it seem like it was working. It was an amazing illusion they created. How is your hand?" I asked.

"Fine. They put that buzzing thing on me again," she said.

"What is that thing? Have you seen it before?" I asked.

"Yes. They use that on us from time to time. I don't know what it does. I keep meaning to ask when it happens, but I keep forgetting to," she answered.

Event 73
Subject: Michelle
Date: 1998
Location: United States

(Comment: Once again, a screen memory is used to create a setting. In this event, the theme was wide ranging and covered many people. What could be a better screen setting for contactees and aliens than a UFO conference?

The day after this event, I posted some of this information in a support group E-mail. Several people wrote back to tell me they had dreams that same weekend about being at a UFO conference or convention.

Unfortunately, because every one of those other reports came from people reporting the events as dreams, without conscious recall, they are not included in this book.

Still, we probably do not need to point out that it is quite a coincidence — if it is a coincidence at all — that I would have such an experience, and other abductees would have similar dreams all on the same weekend.)

I was abducted from my home and brought to a rather large building. It was obviously ET made because of the curving white walls and the strange defused lighting that seemed to be coming from nowhere in particular. There were hundreds of humans walking around. They all seemed excited. They were talking about being at some kind of International UFO conference. Everyone seemed happy.

In the middle of the building was a large arena-like area that looked very much like a human auditorium, with rows of seats and a stage area. I was amazed to watch the people sitting in the auditorium all looking up at the empty stage as if they were listening to a compelling lecture or engrossing movie.

I was told by someone that I had to check in at my hotel room before I was allowed into the lecture hall. So I followed their directions to go to the "hotel". Just outside the building was an area of small cubicles that were separated by curtains that hung about six and a half to the ground.

Inside of some of these cubicles were beds, dressers and other things. Some were empty. Most were shared between two or more people. I was instructed to go to the room and change into the clothes provided there and leave anything I had in my pockets there as well. I didn't want to do that because I had my keys and a small amount of money in my pockets. There was no security and I was afraid someone could easily take my things. There were many people coming and going. Most of the curtains were pulled back and you could see other people's things lying around inside the cubicles.

After a short time, I gave in and changed as I was asked. I also bumped into someone I knew from a support group here on Earth. She told me she was excited about going to the UFO conference and didn't seem to see any problem with leaving her things in the curtain-enclosed space.

Inside the conference building again, I walked to the area where people were sitting down looking at the stage. I asked someone at the door what they were watching. He said there were several speakers listed for the night and it should be a great night. Every now and again, I heard someone's name being called over a loud-speaker announcement system. I asked the man at the door what that was all about. He said that they were doing a drawing and if your name was called, you could claim a prize at the office. I shrugged and walked away.

Soon I came to an area where there were many gray aliens and several very hall human looking aliens walking among the crowd. Not one of the human's seemed to notice them. I saw a gray I recognized. I went to him and asked what was going on. He explained by asking me if I didn't believe it was far nicer for the people to believe they were attending a conference even if it wasn't real, rather than to have them sit around, worrying until it was their turn. He and I talked about the pros and cons of the situation for a little while. When my name was called I ignored it and kept talking to the gray. My name was called again.

A woman who recognized me in the crowd came over to me to tell me she heard my name called. I thanked her and told her that I wasn't interested, and that she could go claim my prize. The gray stopped her and told her she could not do that. He told me I had to go myself.

Looking back, she did not react to the gray as if it were anything unusual for her to be talking to him. I do not know if that was in fact the case, or if she did not see him as a gray at all.

I went to the "office" to claim my prize and was asked to sit in a chair. My arms and legs were placed on extensions of the chair and I could not longer move them. A tray like device was placed around my neck so that my chin rested on the device. I could not move my head once this was in place.

A gray opened my mouth and put something in it. I was glad he didn't put anything down my throat. I thought to him, "What are you doing and why?"

He thought back, "We are amending your system. This will protect you."

I asked him what I was being protected from. He looked at me with a quizzical look, as if I should have known. He went on to explain that there was a probability that a good portion of the population would soon be exposed to bacteria that would be resistant to current medications. He said what they were doing would give me some level of healing ability if I was exposed to these germs.

I asked him if all the others were having the same thing done. He said some were, some where having other things done.

When I was released, I saw Hetar. He told me I did good and asked me if I wanted to attend the conference or just go home. I pointed out that the conference wasn't real anyway, and asked to go home, so he took me home.

Event 74
Subject: Adult Female
Date: 1996
Location: United States

(Comment: The following account illustrates another use for screen memories. In this case, the subject is not the one experiencing the screen, but rather is the one who is being screened to appear as someone she is not.

We received many reports from contactees who reported that other contactees saw them as different individuals during certain abduction events. In most cases the reason for the disguise was obvious.)

The subject reported that she was on shipboard. She was sitting in a rounded room with benches coming from the walls. There was an elderly woman there. The subject tried to talk to the woman, but the woman just mumbled what sounded to the subject to be the rosary prayers in Spanish and ignored her.

After a short while, two small gray beings came into the room and the woman started to cry in Spanish. She didn't want to go with them.

One of the gray beings telepathically asked the subject to accompany the elderly woman, so the subject did.

Inside the examination room, the subject was positioned so that the old woman could easily see her. The woman grabbed the subject's hand and started to call her Santa Maria.

The old woman held the subject's hand and prayed. The subject said she realized that the elderly woman thought she was the Virgin Mary. She reported feeling very uncomfortable about this. She tried to explain to the woman that she wasn't Santa Maria. The woman did not seem to hear her words, or didn't understand them. The subject reported that she believed the elderly woman thought she was speaking words of reassurance.

The gray being telepathically told the subject, "If it gives her comfort to see you as she needs to see you, then what harm does it do?"

The subject was not sure she was pleased about the deception, but realized that the old woman was drawing comfort from the fact that she believed she was holding the hand of the Virgin Mary.

The subject decided not to fight it. Instead, she stroked the old woman's forehead and helped to comfort her as a procedure was done on her. The subject said she was overcome with a strong feeling of joy in helping the old woman, and believed that she gained some understanding about screen memories and how they are used.

Section 4.2 Apocalyptic Visions

By far, visions of some great catastrophe destroying the Earth are not only the most common that contactees experience, they are also the most publicly recognized by the media and researchers. Even in the contactee community, speculation runs wild as to when, why and how these catastrophes will unfold, though most believe they are going to happen sooner or later.

You only have to watch a few television shows or read a few books on alien abduction to know that contactees are continually shown visions of great floods, raging fires, atomic war and meteors striking the Earth. Few outside the abductee community know that the aliens are not just showing their subjects these things, but they are also giving them opportunities to practice surviving such things.

This practice of survival skills often comes in the form of apocalyptic visions. Because many of these visions are reoccurring, reports in this section do not have a date. Instead they are labeled "on-going".

Event 75
Subject: Adult Female
Date: On-going
Location: United States
(Comment: In this vision, the person is compelled to go to a particular place. When they get there they find it was one of only a few safe places they could reach in time.)

The subject reported that she was brought into a small room by a group of aliens that consisted of both tall and short grays and abnormally tall human looking beings. They made her sit in a chair and she began to drift into a vision provided for her.

In this vision, the subject found herself compelled to drive her car as quickly as she could to a mountainous region about two hundred miles from where she lives. She then drove up a mountain access road on one of the peaks. Once on top, she turned and looked down at a lake. Around the lake, for as far as she could see was only wilderness.

She peered into the distance in an attempt to find some sign of a town nearby, when without warning, the distant horizon flashed brightly, then burst into flames. She reported that the flames looked to be in the direction of her home.

Once again, without any forewarning, the whole mountain began to shake, and the ground under the great lake opened up, causing the lake to pour into the Earth. In a moment's time, it is gone, leaving the subject looking at the now empty lake bed and the smoke and flames on the horizon.

Event 76
Subject: Adult Male
Date: On-going
Location: United Kingdom
(Comment: Is this an alien version of duck and cover? Many contactees are told that if they can only live through a nuclear blast, they will be "fixed" or cured of any radiation problems. But surviving the blast is paramount.)

The subject reported he was once again in a vision provided by the aliens. He was suddenly aware that he was riding on a bus. There were a lot of people there who he did not know. Sometimes his son was there with him. His son was always about seven years old in the vision, regardless of the fact that he was now a teenager. The bus was driving along a highway toward London, even though the subject did not live anywhere near London.

The subject reported that he was overcome with an uneasy feeling. He looked toward the city skyline. Far in front of the bus, he saw a bright flash and then a mushroom cloud. He knew that there was a nuclear explosion in London.

He reported his first reaction was panic, then he realized that there would soon be flash-over and a percussion wave that would bring deadly radiation with it. When the vision included his son, he would grab the child stuff him under the seat of the bus, then place myself over the boy to protect him. They would then wait, in horrible silence, while the wave approached.

The subject reported that the wait seemed like it took forever, but it was only moments before the shock wave hit. When it did, he woke up to find himself sitting up on a table in the company of aliens. He was terrified and panicked by the vision, because it was so real that when he was in it, he did not know it was just a vision.

Event 77
Subject: Michelle
Date: On-going
Location: United States
(Comment: Much the same as the previous account, this is another common type of "duck and cover" experience. Nuclear blast experiences are not limited to one country.)

This is one of a series of apocalyptic visions I have been made to experience over the years with the ETs. In this particular vision, I am always driving my car down a highway. It's rush hour and my children are in the car with me.

Far in the distance, I see a bright flash and I know that someone just dropped a nuclear bomb on Boston. I have no doubt of this fact. So I drive between the traffic as fast as I can to get near a highway overpass bridge. I then grab my children, get out of the car and run to get behind the earth and stone wall of the overpass so that the it is between us and the blast, heat and shockwave of the nuclear explosion.

I put my children down on the ground and lay over them to protect them. I command them, in a very loud voice, that no matter what happens they are not to open their eyes until I tell them it is okay to do so. I do not know quite why I say this, except that maybe I believe the flash of the nuclear blast will blind them.

It only takes a few brief moments after we lay on the ground before the shockwave hits us. There is a strange warm wind after. I can almost imagine the hill creating a "wind break" between the blast and my children. I keep repeating to myself, "They can take care of radiation problems, but if you're a pile of ashes, forget it."

After the shockwave passes, the vision ends and I find myself with Hetar on shipboard.

Event 78
Subject: Adult Woman
Date: On-going
Location: United States
(Comment: In this event, the woman and her companion have very different reactions as to how to handle the situation.)

The subject reported the gray aliens subjected her to a reoccurring vision. In the vision she was standing on a sidewalk in a place that was not totally familiar to her. She was walking with someone else.

The subject reported that suddenly she saw a bright flash in her eyes. She was sure it was a nuclear flash, so she had to find a place to "duck and cover" to get away from it. She ran to a house and tried to kick in the basement window in the hopes of finding shelter.

The person with her stood up tall in the coming turmoil and said that they would rather die quickly in the blast than try and survive, only to die later in a much more horrible, slow way.

As the person with her was telling her this, a great, hot wind came and the person standing there vaporized. She said that because she was in shelter, she was not completely vaporized.

At that point she woke up to find herself shaking and sweating in the company of the gray aliens.

The subject explained that on a few occasions she decided not to try and find a place to hide. Rather, she just stood with her friend and allowed herself to be vaporized. Each time she did this, she would awaken to find herself staring directly into the face of a taller being. He always seemed angry at her and she could hear him think to her that she did not react correctly — that she must find shelter.

Event 79
Subject: Teenage Boy
Date: On-going
Location: United States
(Comments: This vision does not involve nuclear destruction. Pay particular attention to the conclusion the abductee draws from this vision. It is not a rare view. Many abductees hold this same view about the end of the world. That is, that they will be saved by the aliens and not be destroyed with the rest of the people on the Earth.)

The subject reported his whole body was numb. He could not move and knew the aliens were in his room. He reported that he always knew when they were in his room because he would hear a strange buzzing in one ear that was different than a regular buzzing in the ear.

He reported that they brought him onto their ship. He was made to lie down on a table and some kind of movie was projected on the ceiling above him. He looked at the movie and soon felt like he was in the movie, not just watching it.

The subject reported the movie was about the *end of the world*. There were huge disasters going on everywhere. There were dead bodies all over the place. There were fires, floods and wars. He said it was as if he saw all that was going on over the whole face of the Earth at one time.

Then he was standing on a beach. He knew that there was a huge tidal wave coming. He could see it approaching over the horizon. It was massive. Bigger than any wave he had ever seen before. The beach in front of him went totally dry, as if the tidal wave was sucking back all the ocean water.

He looked at it with utter horror. He knew it was going to wash over him and kill him. Even if he ran it would overtake him and kill him.

The wave kept coming closer and closer. The subject reported that his fear became stronger and more intense. Then suddenly, he did not feel as scared anymore. He was suddenly overcome with a strong feeling he described as, "I know I'm going to die, but it's ok."

The subject said the wave was very loud. It was towering above his head. He looked up to watch the wave crash down on top of him. Instead, he saw a UFO hovering just over the wave. He then felt his body being sucked up into the UFO.

He said he knew he was saved from the jaws of death.

The subject reported that because of this reoccurring vision provided by the aliens, he believes they are telling him that when the end of the world does come, he will be saved by them for sure.

Chapter 5
Government Involvement

Speculation runs wild when you ask people what they believe the governments of the world know about the alien phenomenon. A recent study done in the United States showed that a majority of people believe the United States' Government is covering up the existence of aliens.

Do the governments of the world really know about aliens, and are they involved in a grand cover-up? You can decide for yourself as you read the following encounters. Pay particular attention to how similar many of the encounters are even though they happened to people from several different countries.

Some people have speculated that with the illusion capabilities of the aliens, many of the encounters that abductees recall, that revolve around human government involvement, are illusions created by the ETs. Others say that there are, in fact, no aliens at all and all the memories are totally a result of military intervention. The latter view became an even more popular theory after the widely watched television show "The X-Files" did a series of episodes in which one of the main characters was abducted, later to find out she was not taken by aliens, but rather by her own government.

Surely, if any government knew about the aliens, they would — if only for national security reasons — want to know who the alien are contacting and why. Would they go as far as to fake abductions or even kidnap their citizens and pretend to be some greater force in order to fulfill this objective? Do they have some sinister plan? Is there something about people being contacted by aliens that makes them different in a way that piques the government's curiosity? Or is the rumor of government involvement (any government, not limited to that of the United States) only that; a rumor.

In the following accounts, you will read things that suggest that governments of several countries know what is going on and may, in fact, be actively involved. But to what degree is anyone's guess at this point. Though the majority of the following accounts come from American citizens, a few came from other countries such as Canada, Great Britain and Mexico. Nevertheless, you will see, they are very similar.

We do not revisit the famous accounts from people who have claimed they were on crashed alien craft and rescued by the military, later to have their memories erased. Nor do we rehash the stories from retired Army and Airforce personnel.

This is not a reflection of our belief in these accounts. It is simply because, as we collected events, we have found encounters we believe you will find much more interesting and ominous. We found common accounts of things that are seldom, if ever, spoken of, or written about.

We have found similar encounters occurring across the United States, and the world. The few who reported these events were ignored by the media at large. Maybe this was because the implications of the information in these accounts are staggering. Maybe it is simply because they are so amazing that until you hear the same kind of accounts from several disconnected, unrelated sources, you cannot bring yourself to believe them.

Did the government of the United States do a complete census of all Americans who have had contact with extraterrestrials? If you believe the accounts of rational, educated, people who were fully conscious at the time of their experience as they were counted and logged by the United States Government in 1996, then you have to believe that it is possible. Many remember it happening to them, some of those stories follow.

But, there is always that doubt. Could this all be an elaborate ET game? After all, we know they have the ability to make us see things differently from what they are. They have a power of illusion over us when we are with them. Could the events these people recall be only a creation of the aliens for their own ends? Whose motives are more likely? Who stands to benefit from such an event and in what way? These are all questions for you to explore if you choose to. We chose only to give you the accounts we have found that may help you along the way.

As you read on, know that the following are from several sources. Most subjects do not know any of the other subjects who related similar events. No event witnesses were given any briefing, material or prompting in any way that would lead them. We believe you will find the events they endured far more revealing than any of the stories you may have heard a hundred times already in UFO literature or on TV.

We should also point out, these events are presented to you as they were presented to us. We are not making any judgment on what any government may or may not have done, nor are we making any speculation as to why, if true, these people were subjected to these procedures by their human, co-inhabitants of planet Earth.

Section 5.1 Abductee Census

In 1996, over a period of several weeks, abductees all over the United States began talking about vivid dreams they had of being brought to barbecues, company picnics and bingo games. This is not particularly strange. After all, people dream about such things. But, how many dream that the barbecue or picnic is being held in an underground facility and that you must pass military guards who require your social security number in order to let you in?

The following four accounts document only four contactees' experiences with what appears to be, for all intents and purposes, a census of all American alien abductees by the Government of the United States.

Assuming the United States Government does know and interact with alien visitors to planet Earth, it would only make sense that they would want to know, for various reasons, which of their citizens were directly involved with the aliens. To do that, they would need to perform some kind of census.

Considering the state of the relationship between the world governments and UFOlogy, it is unlikely that any government would admit they took a census of contactees.

You are free to decide what you want to believe. Did it really happen, or was it an alien illusion. Maybe there is a third explanation for the following four events that we have not explored here.

Event 80
Subject: Adult Male
Date: 1996
Location: United States

(Comment: This first of four events comes from an X-military man. Notice how the subject backs down as soon as a gray alien enters the scene.)

The subject reported he was with his wife and family. His daughters were walking in front of him and his wife was at his side. His son was talking to someone not far from him. They walked to a gated area. The subject kept staring a man who was standing at the gate. The subject watched as the man checked off people's names when they went into the gate area.

His daughters thought the man was dressed as a clown. They thought the family was going to some kind of party or picnic. The subject had his doubts. Something about it didn't seem right to him. The men who his daughters thought for sure were clowns were not. The subject reported they were dressed as marines.

When he got to the head of the line, the subject asked the man for his name and rank, because he was an X-military man himself.

The uniformed man replied, "Sir, you must be mistaken. I am not in the Armed Forces."

The subject felt his answer was too formal for a clown. This made the subject sure the man was in the Armed Forces.

The uniformed man told the subject he needed everyone's social security number so the family could get into the event.

The subject didn't want to give him the numbers. He reported that as he talked to the uniformed man, he saw a gray alien standing behind him.

The gray looked at the subject and he could not help but tell the man the social security numbers of everyone in his family.

Event 81
Subject: Adult Female
Date: 1996
Location: United States

(Comment: In this second example, the woman was more than happy to give your social security number to the man at the gate.)

The subject reported that she was sure she was about to be abducted by aliens when she woke up in her bed and felt the strong sensation of being watched. She tried to get up but heard a very strong forceful voice say, "Stay down." So she did.

She felt as if she were floating. Right away, she recognized that floating feeling as one she often had during abduction events. Because of this, she expected to see gray beings when she opened her eyes.

When she finally opened her eyes, she was surprised to find herself standing at the top of a long flight of stairs. She was surrounded by people. She was sure they were co-workers from her day job, but few of them looked familiar to her at all. She believed she was going to a company picnic and was thinking it was a nice break from work.

She walked down the four flights of stairs to the ground floor. There she headed for the gate that she believed led to a dining hall. Before we went in, she was stopped by a man who was standing at a turnstile. He said he had to verify that she was with the company and needed her social security number.

She gave it to him willingly and he appeared to be looking it up and checking it off on the list he had. Then she passed him and went into a big room, where she sat at a long table. After some time she began to wonder when the food was coming. She was annoyed because she was hungry.

Her memory faded at this point. The next morning she woke up in her home.

Event 82
Subject: Michelle
Date: 1996
Location: United States
(Comment: In this event, Michelle experienced the census first hand, with full consciousness and recall.)

I was on shipboard with Hetar. There were a lot of people there, many more than usual. Everyone was talking. They seemed happy and excited. Most were talking about going to a barbecue or company picnic. My friend, Gene, was there, too. He was lost in a screen memory just like the others around me. He believed he was going for some kind of job fair that was being held along with a free barbecue.

Actually, I found it quite amusing.

Hetar came in. He was accompanied by many grays, both small and tall. The people didn't seem surprised or afraid of them at all. It was as if they did not see them as aliens.

The grays started to lead the people into one of two large doorways that led to white, expandable walkways with metal floors. These tube-like walkways looked just like the kind used by humans to board airplanes.

I asked Hetar what they were doing. He told me that there had been an agreement with the United States Government. He said that as part of the agreement, the ETs had to bring all their United States resident contactees to this place to be counted and noted.

I asked why they wanted to do that. Hetar explained that the United States gave the excuse that they were protecting their citizens and needed to see each contactee to make sure they were in good health and not abused by the aliens.

I told Hetar that I did not want to go and be counted.

He said I did not have to because they already knew who I was from my book and my work in the public. He said it was not necessary that I go, but the others around me had to.

I looked at Gene. I figured that I should probably go with him and see what would happened. When it was Gene's turn to go through the tube-like walkway, I followed along.

The walkway led to a landing at the top of a very large set of stairs that went down four flights. The room the stairs were in was huge. The ceiling above my head was made of I-beams that were painted a rusty red color. The stairs appeared to be concrete in a metal framework. They were about 15 feet across with one central railing in the middle. The edges of each step were metal and painted yellow. The railing was black. Each flight had a landing before the next flight. There were walls lining both sides of the steps.

Hundreds of people were walking down the stairs. They were all happy and laughing. Many of them talked about how great it was that they were going to a free barbecue. It was amazing how convinced they were.

From behind me, an older fellow called out, "Hey, Michelle!" I recognized the voice and turned. I knew him from many events. I called him "Papa". He was walking with his arms around two younger ladies. They all seemed so happy. He waved at me. The women smiled. He said something about eating a whole rack of ribs, which I found unusual because I thought he was a vegetarian. We exchanged waves and words, then I turned back around.

The line was moving slowly and I was only about halfway down the steps. Gene was talking about how great a job he was going to get at this job fair. I decided to see if I could wake him from his screen memory. I asked him how he heard about this job fair we were going to. He said he heard about it in the paper. I asked him why he was not wearing his suit and was going to a job fair dressed in his pajamas. He blushed, then said something about really having a suit on.

I looked around. From where I stood I could easily see that at the bottom of the stairs there were four young men dressed in well pressed army-like uniforms. They were each wearing a hat and holding an electronic clipboard that looked a lot like the kind delivery men carry. They spoke to each abductee, recorded something on the clipboard, then directed the abductee to go through one of four turnstiles behind them. I could not hear what they were asking from where I stood.

Once through the turnstiles, the people were led into one of four rooms. From where I was, I could see that the room on the far left led into an area with a very high ceiling. It appeared as if its walls were made of corrugated metal. The part of the area I could see looked very much like an airplane hanger. I could not see much in the two middle rooms. The doors would be opened, ten or twelve people would be let in and then the doors would be closed again.

In the room on the far right, I could see a low counter with human men dressed in white lab coats standing behind it. The people going into this room were all holding a slip of paper. I do not know where they got the paper. I assumed from the man standing by the turnstile to this room. As they entered the room I could see each one give their slip of paper to the men behind the counter before they walked beyond my sight.

I saw a friend of mine named Denise standing in the row that was leading to this last room. I called to her over the chatter. It was very noisy in the room. It took several shouts before we made contact. She waved to me and told me she was chosen for some prize and was going to play a free game of bingo. She offered to hold a spot for me at the bingo table if I wanted to meet her there. I almost laughed out loud. The screen memory they were under was very strong. Denise has very good conscious recall and generally didn't fall for screen memories. But she was convinced she was in line to play bingo.

By the time we got to the top of the last set of stairs, I had questioned Gene enough about the job fair screen that he was beginning to get edgy. I asked him if he saw the man at the bottom of the stairs and if he knew why he was there. Gene replied that he must be the man taking everyone's registration.

I asked Gene what the man was wearing.

He looked and then said with surprise, "He's wearing a military uniform!"

I said, "Exactly."

Gene said he didn't want to work for the Army and said he wanted to just go home. So we turned around to go back up the stairs. That proved to be impossible to do. The stairs were packed solid with people walking down. There was no room to make our way back up.

174

At the bottom of the stairs I noticed that on our right, the wall ended and the staircase extended beyond it and up back the way we came. I pointed this out to Gene.

When we got to the bottom of the stairs, the young man in uniform politely asked us if we were there for the barbecue. Gene said yes. He asked us if we would kindly give him our social security numbers to verify that we were on the guest list. Gene blurted out his social security number to the young man.

I walked up to the stairs that led up, climbed over the chain and called for Gene to follow me.

The young man called out, "Ma'am, that is not the way to the barbecue. Please, Ma'am. You are entering a restricted area."

I ran as fast as I could up the stairs. Gene followed.

Because of my asthma, I didn't get very far before I had to stop and rest to catch my breath. I thought for sure someone would be following us. But when I turned to look behind me, there was no one there.

Gene and I rested for a short while — no more than twenty or thirty seconds — then we started to walk up the stairs again. We walked to the third floor landing and found a metal door with a small glass window in it. I tried to open the door but it was locked. Through the window I could see a hallway with similar doors on both sides. The hallway ended about forty feet from where I stood.

We continued to the top floor. Just as on the third floor, there was an identical door on the fourth floor. It was also locked. There was another door on the fourth landing. I tried it. It opened. But it opened to the top of the long stairway down. There were so many people still on the stairs that it was useless as an exit. So I just sat down at the top of the stairs and waited.

It was clear that we were at the end of the line. There was no place to go. Still, no one had followed us. We

175

heard some shuffling on the I-beam above our heads. Gene and I looked up. There was a pigeon roosting on the I-beam. It had some kind of white plastic tag clipped on its wing that was causing it to hold it awkwardly. Gene tried to lure it down so he could catch it and take the clip off, but the bird did not want anything to do with us.

We sat there alone and speechless for some time. Gene still seemed unaware of where he was or why. Now he was convinced we were waiting for a subway train. After sometime, Hetar came in through the locked door and told me to stay where I was. When the people had been reloaded, he would come and get Gene and me. So there we sat. Gene chitchatted a bit about nothing much. He was not concerned since he was sure we were just waiting for a subway train.

It seemed to be at least an hour later before Hetar came back to get us. He led us through the other door to the top of the stairs and across the landing to another door that led to a big hallway, then into another tube-like flexible walkway and back onto the ship.

I asked him if it was all done now. He said that particular shipment was done, but there would be many more over the next few days.

In the morning, I called my friend Denise and asked her if she had any memory. She said she did not. I asked her if she had any dreams from the night before. She said she had a dream she was going to a barbecue, which she found strange since she and her family will not eat meat. She also said when she woke up her throat was sore.

Over the next few days I talked to at least ten more abductees who had *vivid dreams* of going to barbecues that week.

Event 83
Subject: Adult Male
Date: 1996
Location: United States (subject not American)
(Comment: It would appear that residents of the United States were not the only ones to be counted. Maybe this subject just happened to be in the wrong place at the wrong time.)

The subject was a foreigner visiting in California at the time. He said he very clearly remembered he was in the company of gray aliens, when his memory started to go strange. Suddenly he thought he was on a human airplane. This was not odd to him since his work requires him to fly a lot.

He believed he was departing from a jet plane at an airport. He walked down a long corridor. When he got out, he was in a very big building. There were many people there. He explained that he followed a crowd of people through the building and down some stairs. When he got to the bottom, he began to look around for someone holding up a sign with his name on it, figuring that his company would have sent a driver. He was wondering where his luggage was. He was concerned because he wasn't quiet sure what airport he was in.

He walked up to a man who was in a dark blue uniform. The subject assumed he was airport security. He asked the man where the airport security office was. The man told the subject he could help him. The man in uniform then pulled out an electronic clipboard and asked the subject for his social security number.

The subject explained he was a foreigner and did not have one.

The uniformed man asked for the subjects name, (Editor's Note: This subject has a very common name, such as — but not — John Smith.)

The subject told him his name, but the uniformed didn't believe him and said, "No, I mean your real name."

He insisted it was his real name. He explained once again that he did not live in the United States.

The man in uniform asked for the subject's visa or passport. The subject reached for his pockets, but found nothing. He tried to explain to the man that he didn't know where his identification was, and that it must be in his luggage. The subject said he was on the verge of panicking because he knew one does not try and cross a country border without identification.

Another person from who he believed was from airport security came over and took the subject to a room where they searched him and questioned him about his identification. He gave them all the identification numbers he could remember from his own country. After a while, the man in uniform led him back onto the same plane he came from. His memory faded at that point. The subject found himself the next morning lying in bed, trying to believe it was all a very long, very vivid dream.

Section 5.2 Kidnapping

One disturbing trend in events we encountered suggested that some abductees were systematically kidnapped by some human-based organization when they were teenagers. Albeit, circumstantial, when asked about unusual events during their teenage years, several people came up with similar reports about being missing without memory of where they had been. Many of them thought that perhaps they were in the hands of the aliens and had experienced missing time. This is possible of course, but our research showed there may be another explanation.

Consider the stories from the following four abductees. Just like the others, they recalled being missing for up to several days. Unlike the others, they had some measure of memory of where they were and what happened during that time.

Event 84
Subject: Teenaged Male
Date: 1976
Location: Canada

(Comment: Could it be that the event below indicates that there has been some kind of systematic plan to test abductees psychic abilities? If the following account was unique we could disregard it, but it is not. There are many such events.

Moreover, these events are not limited to one continent, country or government.

So far, we have not received any similar accounts from contactees who are currently teenagers. In fact, all of the accounts below took place more than twenty years ago.

If such a system existed, is it still in operation? Could it be whoever was controlling these events got what they wanted and the project ended? Could they be using far more sophisticated methods that are untraceable now?

Still, once again, you must consider that there could be an alien illusion at work. For those who tell these stories, there is no doubt. Though the events may have happened because they were contactees, they believe the aliens had nothing to do with it.)

The sixteen year old subject lived with his parents in a posh neighborhood in Toronto. He was walking home late one night, between 11:00 and 12: 00 midnight. He reported that a car pulled up quickly, right behind him. He turned to see what was going on and felt someone reach around behind him and put a hand over his mouth. The subject reported feeling as if the person put a cloth over his mouth as well. Everything went black after that.

When he came to consciousness, he was sitting in a chair in a large, unremarkable room. There were several strange objects in front of him. There were also several men standing around him. The subject reported that the men began to ask questions. They asked him what he knew about UFOs. Despite the fact that the subject reportedly told them very little more than what he had seen on television, they started to lecture him about how UFO occupants could not be trusted.

The subject reported that he began to yell at the men that he didn't know what they were talking about and they were crazy.

The men did not respond.

Finally, he decided that if he agreed with them, they would leave him alone. After the lecture, they instructed the subject to hit a target in front of him. They told him to hit the target with his mind. The subject recalled that the men said if he hit it, they would let him go.

Try as he might, nothing happened when the subject attempted to do what they instructed. The subject reported that the men seemed a bit disgusted and gave up on their questioning. He then felt something prick his shoulder and everything went black.

The next thing he remembered was standing in the exact same place on the road where the car had pulled up behind him. He remembered someone had just put their hand over his mouth. He whirled around to attack the person he believed was behind him, but no one was there.

The subject reported he walked into his house, which was nearby. It was close to 1:30 AM. His memory of the elapsed time became vague and by the morning it seemed as if it were just a dream or a missing time event.

Only after exploring the event as missing time, did the subject realize it was not a dream.

Event 85
Subject: Teenaged Male
Date: 1963
Location: United Kingdom

(Comment: Though the subject of this event does not recall any psychic testing, the event suggests that he may have undergone such testing.)

The subject was a teenager. He and a girlfriend were out at night looking for a place to find some privacy. While they were walking, they noticed that a large dark car was following them. This was very unusual, because in the subjects country large cars were not the norm. They assumed it was either the police, wondering what they were up to, or possibly someone trying to sell drugs, wondering if they were buying.

After a few moments, the car drove up beside them and a man leaned out and asked them if they were interested in buying any drugs.

The subject said he shrugged at them to let them know he was not interested.

Then the man in the car asked the subject for directions to a different part of town. His girlfriend leaned forward toward the car to give the directions and looked into the window. She then got very upset and told the subject they better go. The subject said he did not leave right away, even though his girlfriend ran off.

He said he leaned toward the car to give the directions. When he did, the driver leaned back, and motioned as if he couldn't hear him. So the subject leaned in further. He reported that at that point he vaguely remembered being pulled into the car and struggling. He was overcome with dizziness, then blacked out.

Later, he wakes to find himself draped over the back steps of the building where he lived.

He recalled to us what he described as "very vivid dreams" from that night. In the first, he was tied to some kind of stretcher and put into a van. In the second, he was in some kind of hospital. There were human doctors around him. They had him wired up to a machine that looked, much like a modern EEG machine that measures brain waves.

He reported that the day after the event with the car he saw his girlfriend again. The subject demanded to know where she went and what happened. He reported that she told him she returned for him but he was gone, she assumed with the men. She explained that she ran away because, she said, "There was something queer about the guys in the car."

Event 86
Subject: Teenaged Male
Date: 1978
Location: United States

(Comment: In the following event, the subject describes a birdcage-like instrument placed over his head. Could this have been some kind of faraday cage?

Though the subject of this event is once again a teenaged male, it does not indicate that only males were subjected to this testing. There were reports from females, but we were not given permission to use any herein.)

The subject was 17 years old. At about 10 p.m. one night, he was walking alone from a friend's house when a dark sedan approached him. There were three men in the car. One of them asked him directions to a road in town. When he leaned over to hear the man, he was grabbed from behind.

The next thing he recalled was being half awake in the dark. He believed he was in an ambulance and that he had been in an accident and was on his way to the hospital. There was something over his head. It was hard and metal. The subject described it as being made like a birdcage. It covered his whole head. His hands were tied down, crossing at the wrist. They were put up around his neck so that they, too, were covered by the cage-like restraint. He was unable to talk. He wondered what kind of accident he was in that he needed to be in what he believed was a traction device. He blacked out again.

The subject reported that the next thing he recalled was being helped to sit up in some kind of doctor's office. The furniture was all white and stainless steel. The people who helped him sit up were both dressed like doctors with white coats. There was also a woman dressed in a dark, navy blue uniform.

The subject reported the woman started to ask him questions like what was his name; where did he live; and if he remembered how he got there.

The cage like device was still over his head and hands. He asked her why he had it on. She told him that it was for his own protection. She said that she would take it off if he promised he would control himself. She had a man take the cage off his head. His hands were allowed to rest on his lap, but they did not untie them.

The subject figured he was in some kind of jail, so he told the woman that he wanted to know what he was being charged with and told her he knew he had the right to a phone call.

The subject said the woman started to question him about UFOs and aliens. He was confused because at the time, he did not know he was an abductee.

She told him that the aliens lied to him and that by keeping the alien confidences and secrets he was betraying mankind. She pointed out that if the aliens really cared about the subject they would not let him be kidnapped in the first place. The subject was sure that she used the word kidnapped. The subject said the woman lectured him about the aliens, saying they did not care about humans and did not believe in God. It was his duty to country and to the human race to tell her what he knew. He insisted he knew nothing.

She shouted at the subject and accused him of betraying humankind. Then she walked out.

The subject reported that after the woman left, two men walked in, dressed in suits. The shorter one had on a black suit. The taller one had on a dark gray suit. The shorter man spoke first. He said they had a few things they wanted to talk to him about. They said they had a great job to offer him if he could prove to them that he could handle it. They said they were looking for special people to do special work for them. They explained if the subject took the job, he would be given a new identity, his own house and a generous salary.

They talked to the subject about how *grown up* and *mature* he was, and how nobody understood him at home, and that it would serve them right if he took the job and never went back there.

It was clear to the subject, looking back, that they were trying to appeal to that side of every teenager that thinks he or she is an adult.

The subject said they made promises of power, sex, and money. The subject reported that he didn't believe the men. He said he could barely believe the event was happening at all.

When he did not agree to their offers, the taller man said, "Forget this one. He's too stupid. He's just not the right material for what we need."

The subject broke in and said, "I'm not stupid! What do you need anyway?"

The taller man said, "Never mind. You probably couldn't even hit the target."

The new tactics worked. "What target? Hit it how?" the subject eagerly asked, hoping to prove himself.

They led the subject to a room and showed him some lights on a table. There were two metal circles embedded in the tabletop. They asked him to touch the circles. When he did, the lights lit. Then they asked him to touch just one of the circles and use his mind to make the lights illuminate.

He understood what they wanted because he was a fan of shows about ESP and related topics. So he tried to concentrate on the lights and some of the lit.

The subject turned to the men and asked, "So, do I get the job?"

One man answered, "Not yet. There is one more test."

They handcuffed the subject and led him outside to an area around the building. The subject reported it was sandy and dry like a desert. The area was surrounded by a tall fence.

The tall man pointed to an object that stood in an open area beyond the fence. It was a huge, black, metal object. The subject said it appeared to be more than five stories in height. At the time, the subject thought it looked like a black, metal Ferris wheel with a bowl attached to it. Now the subject believes it was some kind of dish antenna. The subject said its size was impressive, even by today's standards. It terrified him.

The short man once again started to praise the subject about how smart and grown up he was, and how it would be a shame if he had to go back home and live like a 17-year-old again. The man talked about the money and the freedom in very seductive ways.

Then the tall man pointed to the antenna-like object and told the subject, "All you have to do is activate the objective and you have the job."

The subject was overcome with fear. He felt like there was an inner voice screaming from his insides, telling him not to do it. He became afraid and tried to break away, but his hands were still cuffed behind his back and the tall man held him firmly by the elbows.

The subject refused to hit the target. Instead, he started to scream that they were crazy and he wanted to go home.

The subject reported that at that point, the short man became very mean and told him if he did not try and hit the target they would kill him.

The subject did not even know how, or if, he could hit the target, but he knew that he should not do it. Yet, if he did not try he had no doubt they would have killed him. So, the subject pretended to try and hit the target. Nothing appeared to happen.

They told the subject to concentrate and try again. He pretended to try. Before he was done, he felt something jab his right arm. The subject turned to find one of the men had just injected him with something. The subject got very dizzy.

The next thing the subject was aware of, he was lying on the front porch of his Aunt Diane's house. She lived on the outskirts of the town where he lived. She was not home.

The subject reported feeling sick and going to the bushes to throw up. He was too sick to walk home, so he waited for his aunt to come home from work. When she did, she brought the subject inside, gave him something to eat and let him shower. She called his parents and they came to pick the subject up. That is when the subject discovered that he had been gone for three days. His parents assumed he ran away.

He could not tell them where he was. He did not have more than a dream-like memory of the whole event until years later when it came back to him with vivid detail.

Event 87
Subject: Child Male
Date: 1959
Location: United Kingdom
(Comment: The last event in this section describes an unusual event that is similar to several we have received over the years.

Though not apparent on the surface, we believe this could be an example of human intervention with abductee children.

We have found that many life long experiencers have undergone such testing as children. The testing always involves psychic abilities — such as guessing what is in a sealed envelope. Our research suggests that the non-abductee population was not subjected to these types of events.)

The subject, who has a life long history of alien contact, reported that when he was in school, at about age eleven, he was taken out of class by some people he never saw before and never saw after that. He was led to a separate room in the school.

The room he was led to had been changed. Rather than school desks, it had what appeared to be a dentist's chair mounted in the center of the room. He was asked to sit in the chair.

The people first performed a physical examination on him. Then they gave him a card with about twenty symbols on it. He was told it was an intelligence test. He was to try and find a pattern in the card. He was told he had to cross off the symbols he thought made up a pattern, but the correct pattern was on another card that was in an envelope on a desk across the room.

The subject said the instructor told him something to the effect of, "This pattern is very hard to figure out, unless you're some kind of mind-reader. Then you could see through the envelope and figure out what the pattern is." It was as if he wanted the subject to try and "mind read" the pattern.

Once he chose a pattern, they told him the next test was an also an intelligence test. They had him guess if the photograph that was in an envelope put in front of him was of a person, place, or thing; and if possible, could he tell what that person, place or thing looked like? The subject recalled asking how he was supposed to know that. He was told if he was smart enough he would figure it out. So he did his best, because he did not want to fail the test.

He said he was never given any results to any of these tests.

Chapter 6
Alien Intervention

In this final chapter, we will examine several examples of times when aliens apparently intervened directly in a human subject's Earth life. Here you will find reports of aliens saving lives or healing sickness. We will also look at a few examples of people who have tried to resist their contacts as well as a few stories of times when aliens apparently made mistakes.

Some people may argue that if any aliens go out of their way to save a human subject's life, then it is solely for the alien's own selfish reason. This argument has some validity, as it would lend an explanation to why some abductees are cured or saved, while others are not.

Some contactees believe the aliens have intervened on their behalf because they — as individuals — have an ultimate mission to perform. Others have reported being saved or cured by alien intervention who do not believe themselves to have an important or outstanding role to play in either the alien agenda or their human life. Many others believe they were cured or saved because the aliens cared about their well being.

Do aliens truly care about their human subjects? The question causes heated emotions. For every one person who says they do, there is another who says they do not. Examples of encounters can be interpreted with a slant to reinforce the opinion of whatever side of the question the teller is on.

Of course, the perception of the person having the experience will have a lot of do with whether events are interpreted as positive or negative.

Section 6.1 Resistance

There are countless stories of alien resistance. Many people go through periods where they struggle and fight back against their alien contacts. It does not take much hunting to find stories about people tossing alien bodies out of windows, tales of young men snapping aliens' necks, and anecdotes of people praying and invoking the name of Jesus, thus making the aliens hightail it back to space.

Unfortunately, these types of tales are not likely to be accurate or even true. This it not to say that the people reporting them are lying or purposely trying to deceive. It is simply that they may be misled by other circumstances.

Take for example stories from people who claim to mutilate, strangle or otherwise kill aliens. These things do not happen. People with any dangerous tendencies — and even some who do not have them — are rendered totally and completely immobile when the aliens are near, so that violent episodes cannot happen.

Most people probably do not know it, but it is an extremely common scenario for the aliens to subject angry individuals who would likely attack them if given the opportunity, to reaction test vision in which they are allowed to play out their fantasy of killing aliens. The individual is put into a controlled, alien environment, and made to believe they woke in their room to find the aliens present. The aliens watch the subject's reaction to see if they are dangerous, and to what extent.

On other occasions, we have seen people who have memories of attacking aliens undergo regression therapy only to find out that the event they believed was an attack, was in fact, some kind of screen memory put in place while they were abducted and worked on by the aliens.

It is not uncommon for people who once reported "killing" aliens with their bare hands, to later realize that it was a screen memory or reaction test.

As for people who claim they have "cast out" aliens by invoking the name of Jesus or another deity, some fall under the above explanation. Others could have a more sinister problem.

It must be pointed out that aliens are not demons or angels. They are physical beings. If invoking the name of Jesus, God, or some other deity causes them to flee, then one has to consider that the beings that fled were not aliens, but some other type of being disguising themselves as aliens.

It is not our intention to get into a long lecture on the difference between aliens and demons. Nor is it our intention to discredit anyone's belief in the power of their God to save them from things they find distasteful. As a matter of fact, it is not even a reflection of our own belief in God.

We simply offer the reader what we have observed. That being, people who claim they can make alien contact stop by invoking the name of God, often tell stories of the aliens they see being surrounded by the smell of human waste, strong evil feelings and telekinetic havoc.

If this is in fact what they are experiencing, then we simply suggest that they are not dealing with aliens, but with something else.

In the following three events, you will not read about people snapping alien heads off like lollipops, or of people throwing holy water and crystals at the beings, thus making them scream in terror and run. You will read first hand, conscious accounts of how people resisted the aliens in ways that you might find unusual.

What you might find even more unusual, is how the ETs responded in return.

Event 88
Subject: Michelle
Date: 1996
Location: United States

(Comment: This was an unusual event for me. I am not one to threaten anyone, but at the time, I was so frustrated.)

I was lying in bed. It was about 3:00 a.m. in the morning. I could not sleep because my daughter's pet mouse was running in its mouse wheel and the wheel squeaked. I was too tired to get up and do anything about it though, so I just lay there awake.

I got the sense that the ETs were nearby. I had been feeling very annoyed with them for several months because I wanted a particular answer to a question I was not getting. I heard one approach my bed. I could feel him standing by my side and I could smell the unusual scent their bodies have. I knew it was one of the small ones, because the taller ones seldom ever come into my home.

I peeked through my eyelashes. The room was filled with blue light and there was a small gray alien standing by my bedside. He was holding a small control wand.

I sprang up quickly and grabbed him by the arm, then took the wand from his hand. I put the wand to his forehead and told him that I wanted answers and I knew how to use the wand.

He seemed quite upset. He told me that he did not have any answers to give me, and that I would have to talk to his superiors if I wanted answers. I told him I did not believe him and I was going to use the wand to zap him if he did not give me the answers I wanted.

He tried to talk calmly. He told me that Hetar wanted to talk to me and that was why he was there. He said he was instructed to "collect" me and bring me to see Hetar. He told me that he didn't know anything and begged me to release him and give him back the wand. I refused.

I told him I needed to know why they only let some people remember. He told me he could not answer me. Then he got very quiet and said, "They are coming now."

Before I could respond, there was a flash of white light and two taller grays were standing in the corner of my bedroom. I blurted out, "I need answers. Someone is going to give me answers!"

One of the taller grays opened his hand and something small and round fluttered out of it. It almost looked like a white butterfly. It floated in the air. I thought to myself, "Oh no. Now I'm in trouble."

The white object landed on my forearm and pricked my skin like it was giving me some kind of injection. I looked down at it just long enough to see it was round, about an inch and a half in diameter, and had two black dots on it, giving it the appearance of a button, before I blacked out.

Next think I was aware of, I was laying on an examination table in one of the small, rounded rooms with a catwalk around the top. Hetar was there. He was staring into my eyes. We talked. I cannot recall now what we talked about. I was still feeling very drugged up by whatever was injected in me by the button-like device.

The rest of the contact event was hazy and distorted as if the drug they used to collect me never fully wore off. I remembered being brought home and crawling into my bed. Daylight was just breaking and I was very tired.

The next time I was abducted, the same small gray came to me and woke me. I was very surprised that I was not paralyzed after what I had done the previous visit. I assumed they would have paralyzed me so I would not do it again.

I even asked the gray, "Why didn't you stun me?"

He answered, "You promised not to do it again. I trust you. Besides," he added, "your kind are emotionally flighty. We make allowances for this."

Event 89
Subject: Adult Male
Date: 1993
Location: Mexico
(Comment: This man had an unusual way of trying to discourage of his abductors. Notice how they turned the tables on him. Based on the accounts of others who have done such things and not been subjected to any alien retribution, and knowing the alien sense of humor, their intention could have been more to return the joke than to punish. Yet we cannot know either way as we are not aliens. This is in the category of "not a good idea.")

The subject was angry at the aliens and wanted to get back at them. He said he wanted to shock them in much the same way they shock him. So every night for some time he slept with a cloth sack tied to his body. In it, he kept a large non-venomous snake.

One night, he was abducted and he pulled out the snake. When he did, the small gray beings in the room let out a high pitched screeching sound and ran out of the room. The taller gray there looked at him, and telepathically projected the idea that he was upset by what the subject did.

The subject's memory of that particular event became hazy at that point.

Later that month, the subject recalled being abducted again. This time, he was led into a room that was filled with snakes of all types and sizes. He was made to sit in that room for some time before he was returned home.

He was not a man who was afraid of snakes, yet the shear number of snakes around him made him feel uneasy. He reported saying he was glad he didn't try and scare them with a spider.

Event 90
Subject: Adult Female
Date: 1993
Location: United Kingdom
(Comment: This subject actually ran at and tried to attack a craft. The aliens' response to her effort was unusual to say the least.)

The subject lived in a secluded, country setting. She was home alone because her husband was away on business. One night, she looked out the window and saw a light in the backyard. She panicked because she was afraid it was a UFO. But when she looked outside again she thought it was only a carnival ride in the backyard. After a few moments, she realized that there should not have been a carnival ride in the backyard and she reasoned it must have been a screen memory.

She became very angry. She opened the backdoor and ripped out a shrubbery near the door and began to swing it wildly at the light, shouting for it to go away. Everything went black for her. She remembered nothing until the next morning, when she woke up in bed with her day clothes on.

She remembered what happened the night before and ran to the backdoor to see what she could find in the backyard. When she opened the door, she found that all the shrubs in her backyard had been pulled up and piled against the backdoor.

More than being upset with the idea that she had been abducted, she was now infuriated that they ruined the expensive landscaping of her backyard.

Section 6.2 Mistakes

Many abductees are quick to blame any physical problem they have on a mistake made by the aliens. Nevertheless, the fact is there is little evidence of them actually making mistakes, but there is some proof that mistakes are made.

The next events are examples where the aliens made simple mistakes in organization. These types of mistakes could explain a common event in most abductees lives.

Many abductees are prone to loosing things only to find them in places where they should not (and in many cases could not) have been.

It is not uncommon for an abductee to put an object of value down in the usual spot (for example, keys on a keyhook) only to find it missing the next morning. Later that day, or week, it will show up again on the floor of the shower or some other odd place.

We know of at least two individuals who woke up with rings missing from their hands. Both searched their bedrooms for their rings. Both found nothing. One found her ring laying on top of her television set in the livingroom the next morning. The other — whose ring was far too tight to fall off on its own — found her ring in an ashtray next to her sofa. She was adamant that she didn't take it off, saying that she never took it off since it was her wedding ring.

These types of lost and found games happen to abductees all the time. Could they be a result of aliens loosing track of what belongs to who when they strip abductees down for medical work?

Also consider that these seeming mistakes may be the aliens attempts — albeit not very good attempts — at giving contactees individual proof of their experiences.

Event 91
Subject: Michelle
Date: 1979
Location: United States
(Comment: The following two events illustrate mismanagement of clothing. Although this event upset me because I had an attachment to the clothing involved, it did give me a strong sense of the reality of my experience at a time in my life when I needed it.)

When I was a teenager, I was a big fan of a band named Queen. I had all their records and a vast collection of T-shirts that displayed photos of the band. I was particularly proud of one such shirt I found in a collectors record shop in Boston. It was extremely rare, and even though it was at least three sizes too big for me, I bought it.

Because it was so large, and because I loved it so much, I use to wear it as a nightshirt. One night when I was wearing it I was abducted by the gray beings and taken on shipboard. While I was there, I underwent a procedure that required me to be undressed. My favorite shirt was put to the side.

I was put to sleep for the procedure and was very hazy after it was over. I didn't mind this, as the procedure involved the flushing of my digestive tract with a hose in my bottom and throat. I was glad I didn't have to be aware during it.

Just before I was returned home, two small gray beings came to me holding a nightshirt. They put it on me and brought me home.

The next morning I was both shocked and infuriated to find that rather than my favorite Queen T-shirt, I was wearing a big, worn, yellow T-shirt with a faded picture of Tweety on it!

I couldn't believe that my shirt was gone. For the next few months, maybe longer, every time I was picked up by the aliens, I demanded they find my shirt and return it to me.

To this day, I have never seen that shirt again.

Event 92
Subject: 2 Child Females (as told by mothers)
Date: 1997
Location: United States

(Comment: The following event was confirmed by two individuals. This makes it even more compelling evidence.)

Woman number one's daughter was a big "Barney" fan. She used to have Barney PJs and Barney T-shirts, even Barney underwear. One night the child took her bath, put on her Barney underwear and pajamas and went to bed.

The next morning she woke up to find that she was wearing white underwear with little blue flowers on it. The mother was amazed and shocked. She had no idea where the underwear had come from. She had nothing in the house even remotely like it. Her daughter had just been potty trained a few months before and the only underwear the child wore were her beloved Barney pairs.

The woman was part of an Internet, abduction support group and posted this very strange event. The next morning she received a reply from another woman.

Woman number two's daughter had woken up with Barney underwear on. She reported that she put her daughter to bed in white undies with blue flowers on them. Her child did not own any underwear with characters of any kind on them.

The women talked to each other on the phone later that day. It was clear the children had somehow exchanged underwear. Neither child remembered anything happening the previous night.

Event 93
Subject: Teenage Female
Date: 1965
Location: United States

(Comment: To this day, the subject reports feelings of injustice surrounding the punishment she received because of an alien mix-up.)

The subject reported that when she was a teenager, her family lived just a few houses down from her cousin's house. She and her cousin were the same age and they looked a lot alike. She reported that it was not uncommon for her to see her cousin when she was abducted by gray beings.

One morning the subject reported that she woke up in her cousin's house, in her cousin's bed. Likewise, her cousin woke in the subject's house, in the subject's bed. The subject said he had a vague memory of being abducted, but was not sure if it were a dream.

Both girls were totally unaware of how they got into the wrong houses. The subject reported that both sets of parents thought that although the girls had never done anything like it before, they must have sneaked out during the night and become intoxicated to come back to the wrong houses. Because of this, both the subject and her cousin were punished.

Event 94
Subject: Child Female (as reported by mother)
Date: 1996
Location: United States

(Comment: Was this truly a mistake, or were the aliens giving in to a child's request?)

The mother of the subject reported that the child, who was four years old at the time, was placed securely in her bed at the usual time. Before the mother went to bed herself, she checked on her child, as was her custom. The child was there, just as she should be.

The next morning, when the mother woke up, she did not find the child anywhere in the house. She became concerned. All the doors were locked and dead-bolted with the type of lock you need a key to open from either side. Her husband was still in bed, so no one had opened any of the doors since the night before. There was no sign of forced entry in any doors or windows.

She called for her child, expecting to find her hiding in a closet or under a bed. After a few calls, the mother reported the child called back from the back porch. The mother looked through the double glass doors to the deck on the back of the house. There, sitting on a gliding swing, was her daughter. She was not hurt.

The mother reported that the sliding glass door was still secure with a stick she put in its track the night before. There was no way the child could have gotten out of the house.

The mother opened the door and asked the child how she got outside. The child replied, "The people let me sleep outside so I could see them fly away."

The mother knew of her husband's abductions, but did not know her daughter was subject to them as well. In disbelief, she asked the child, "What do these people look like?"

The child said, "They look funny, and they can make me fly."

Section 6.3 Rescues

Some people believe, and reports suggest, that reptile-like aliens are very anti-human. Despite this, when we heard of events where someone was saved in a manner that involved physical strength, the alien who intervened was almost always a reptilian-like alien. This suggests that some reptilian-like beings may indeed be working on the pro-human side.

In the following section you will read three accounts of people who were physically saved by alien intervention. The first account involves gray aliens and the last two do not.

When we collected stories of rescues, most were vague. No alien was seen. The contactee simply believed the aliens had something to do with the event.

For example, we received several reports where contactees were suddenly compelled to move quickly or turn their cars sharply. By doing so, they avoided getting into a serious accident.

There were also accounts of people who believed their car turned totally on its own, thus saving them from certain death. They attribute this quick turning to alien intervention.

Some people reported they believe that the little voice in their head that suggested to them to avoid a certain place, road or plane trip was an alien influence.

It is not known if these events are alien controlled in anyway. People who have experienced them, and believe they are, cannot be swayed. Yet, without seeing proof of actually alien intervention, the question remains. This is why we only included accounts where the aliens were clearly involved.

Event 95
Subject: Adult Female
Date: 1995
Location: United States
(Comment: Notice how the alien, in the following account, uses his power to create visions to impress upon the subject a fact that may save her life.)

The subject reported that she had been at a company Christmas party, lost herself in the fun and had too much to drink. She admitted that she liked to drink a bit too much, but this was the first time she did it when she had to drive.

As she started to drive home, she reported that the road kept appearing to swerve in front of her as if it were alive. Looking back, she said that she knew she should have stopped, but she wanted to get home and was to intoxicated to really care.

She saw a bright light she thought was solid in front of her on the road. She swerved to miss it, but her reflexes were not good. Rather then avoiding it she drove into the bright object. Luckily for her, it turned out not to be solid.

She said the car seemed to be spinning. She closed her eyes because she was very dizzy. She opened them to find herself sitting in the company of gray alien beings.

The tall one that she saw most often gave her some kind of liquid to drink. It seemed to neutralize the alcohol in her blood. Within minutes, she was no longer feeling drunk.

The alien began to lecture her about how she could have gotten herself killed. He spoke harshly to her and then caused her to see a vision of her body mangled in a crashed car. Then he showed her a vision of her family identifying her dead body. He even showed her visions of each one of her children going through the pain of loosing her.

She began to cry and apologize. The subject reported that the gray was relentless in his chastisement. He showed her bodies of strangers she could have killed as she drove. He showed her visions of her husband moving on and getting remarried and forgetting her. He showed her visions of her facing a God-like force and explaining why she threw away her life in such a way.

She begged him to stop. He said he could not until he was sure her life would never be in danger in such a way again.

After he was done, he returned her to the car, which was now parked in her driveway. Although she believed she was with the aliens facing a reprimand for several hours, when she entered her home, she found that she had arrived home early. It seemed to her that she was home even earlier than she left work.

The subject reported that she has never had a sip of an intoxicating beverage since that day. She also is adamant that this alien intervention saved her life.

Event 96
Subject: Child Female
Date: 1979
Location: United States

(Comment: In the next event, a reptilian being is the hero. This is quite a switch from the common way they are viewed.

Take particular note of how the next two events are similar, even though they happen in different states and different decades.)

The subject was 11 years old. Her family had an above-ground pool in the backyard. Both parents worked and she and her brother were home alone all summer.

They were forbidden to go into the pool when the parents were at work, but they did anyway.

One day, when the brother was over at a friend's house the subject decided to go for a swim. She wasn't concerned that she could drown because the pool was only four feet deep.

She reported that the pool had an aluminum ladder that surrounded its wall. She was swimming around the ladder, going in and out between the rungs under the water, pretending to be a dolphin in an underwater show.

At some point, the subject said her bathing suit got caught on the edge of the ladder and she was stuck in between the rungs, under the water.

She struggled madly to get her head above water, but could not. She pulled at her suit, but in her panic she could not get it undone. It was firmly set.

The subject said she was overcome with a strange feeling when she knew she would soon gasp in water and drown. She thought about her brother finding her body in the pool and how terrible that would be for him.

Just as she was about to gasp in and swallow her last watery breath, the ladder, with the subject still attached, was lifted out of the pool.

The subject reported that a large hand grabbed her and pulled her off of the ladder, ripping her suit in the process. The hand placed her on the ground by the pool's side.

She looked up in amazement, expecting to see her father or brother, but there before her was what she described as a large creature that looked like a human iguana. She said he had a wide face, with protruding lizard eyes and scales that shined in the day's sun. He spoke in a forceful, deep voice and said, "No more pool!"

The subject reported that she was terrified of the being and screamed. When she did, the being vanished in a flash of light.

Event 97
Subject: Michelle
Date: 1998
Location: United States

(Comment: In the next event, pay particular attention to what the being says before it disappears. It is the same words spoken to the subject of Event 96, in a different State, more than twenty years before.)

I was sitting at home alone. I was working on my computer and eating an english muffin with melted cheese on it. The cheese was a mix of Swiss and mozzarella. It was very chewy. I was home from work because I had a bad headcold, and I my nose was stuffy.

I admit, I wasn't paying very much attention to my breakfast, and more attention on my computer screen while I answered my E-mail. While eating my rather chewing breakfast, my nose stuffed up really badly and I choked. I gasped for air and the cheese I was chewing went down my windpipe. I couldn't breath at all.

I tried to cough out the cheese, but couldn't. I tried to pull it out of my throat with my fingers but could not get a grip on it. I could not breath at all. I began to panic.

I ran toward the kitchen to try and get a spoon in hopes of prying the cheese out of my throat. All I could think of was my children coming back from school and finding me dead on the living room floor.

I ran out into the hall, from my home office and started through the living room to the kitchen. As I did, I ran face to face into a very large being. He had a face very much like a chameleon. His eyes were set off his head on cone shaped lumps, and his skin looked to be scaled. I don't recall much else because I was panicking too much to really take him in. The top of his head was almost touching the ceiling of my living room. I didn't have time to startle before he grabbed me, lifting me right off the floor. He squeezed my chest, dislodging the cheese from my windpipe. The cheese flew onto the floor, and he put me down.

"No more cheese!" he said in a very stern voice that made me shiver to my soul.

Right then, my dog ran up and ate the cheese off the floor. Only one of the beings cone shaped eyes turned to look at the dog. The other still looked straight at me. I turned around to look at the dog as well. When I turned back the being was gone. There was no sound, no flash of light; nothing.

At that point, I collapsed onto the living room floor. I don't think I moved for more than twenty minutes. I shuttered every time I thought about it for days after. Later, I wondered why such a being would be sent to save my life.

Whatever the reason, and despite my fear, I have to admit I am glad it was.

Event 98
Subject: Adult Male
Date: 1996
Location: United States
(Comment: Many abductees feel the aliens have a near to constant involvement in their lives. They believe the aliens

know where they are and what they are doing at all times, perhaps because of implants.

The following account comes from such a person who claimed the aliens saved his life. Although there were no aliens actually seen, the events suggest that they could have indeed had a hand in his good fortune.)

The subject reported he was driving home on a highway through a foggy valley. He could barely see the cars in front of him. The only vehicle he could see was a small box van with a local company's logo on it. It drove directly in front of him. The traffic was moving rather fast, regardless of the lack of visibility.

All of a sudden, he realized that the traffic in front of him came to a full stop. He skidded to stop, but it was obvious he was not going to make it.

The subject then reported that everything around him turn a bright blue color. It lasted for several seconds. He could hear cars crashing in front of him, but still had not hit anything.

The light left as suddenly as it came. The subject then realized that his car was at a complete stop, though he did not remember the actual moment it stopped. Moreover, the subject now heard skidding coming from behind him. He was now in the front of a long line of cars that had collided on the highway. He was sure he was behind that line and heading into it, full speed, just moments before.

The subject felt a strange sense of disorientation for a short moment. After that, he ran to the crashed cars to help aid the people in distress.

Before he was ready to leave, the fog passed. He looked at the long line of crashed cars. The subject reported that all the lanes of the highway were blocked by disabled vehicles, and toward the end of the line was the box van he was behind before he saw the blue light fill his car.

Section 6.4 Cures

It is not uncommon to hear stories in the abductee community about contactees who were very sick, even terminal, only to find out later that all signs of their illness are gone without a trace.

This happened to an abductee friend of Michelle's just as we were writing this book. A CAT scan showed the woman had a brain tumor, two weeks later she had her pre-surgery MRI and it showed no sign of anything abnormal. All her blood tests were now normal as well. Was this an act of God? Was it an act of alien intervention?

Most contactees who have had these types of miraculous cures happen in their lives wonder if they could truly be alien intervention, as there is seldom any proof that aliens were involved. Some, however, know without a doubt that aliens had something to do with their cures because they remembered the aliens being involved.

The following are two accounts that are very typical of the kinds of events people reported who saw aliens in connection with their sicknesses being cured.

It would be nice to think that all abductees who get sick will be cured by aliens, but that is simply not the case. Who is chosen to be cured and why is something only the aliens seem to know.

Just as with the life saving interventions, people who were cured do not always feel they are someone special who deserved special attention, although they were seldom sorry it happened.

Event 99
Subject: Teenage Male
Date: 1963
Location: United Kingdom

(Comment: This event is typical. Often when a cure happens in the hospital and the subject recalls seeing the aliens, they will have an open conversation with the beings. Sometimes the aliens even tell the subject why they are curing them.)

The subject was very sick and in the hospital with pneumonia. He thought maybe he was going to "die and go to heaven." One night, what he believed at the time was an angel, appeared at the foot of his bed. He now believes — based on subsequent experiences — that it was an alien in the form of bright light.

The subject, who was told by his parents that he might not get better after all, believed it was an angel to bring him to heaven.

The being standing at the foot of his bed said, "You can't die."

The subject said, "It's okay. If I die, I'll go to heaven. I know it."

The being said, "You can't die. And your lungs are going to be better because you have to sing about the word."

The subject asked, "What's the word?"

The being said, "The word is love."

He asked, "When am I going to sing about it?"

The being replied, "When the time comes." Then the being was gone.

The next morning the subject was so much better, he was released from the hospital within two days.

Event 100
Subject: Adult Male
Date: 1974
Location: United States

(Comment: Could this subject have been taken to an alien craft to have his liver damage repaired? Could they have even replaced his liver? If their intent was to cure the subject, why didn't they remove all traces of the virus that damaged his liver in the first place?)

When the subject was in his twenties, he contracted a sever case of hepatitis. He did not know how sick he was and thought he had a bad case of the flu. Because of this, he avoided treatment until he was so sick he had to go to the hospital by ambulance. By the time he got there, he was almost completely unable to move and his skin, eyes and even fingernails were yellow.

The subject was admitted to the hospital. Tests were done and his parents were told his liver was so damaged he would need a transplant in order to survive. It did not look good for him.

After several days in the hospital, he was laying in his bed when he saw several gray aliens walk into the room and start to touch him. He felt paralyzed. He wondered if they were some kind of hallucination or maybe he was dead and they were some kind of "nether-world beings" come to take him away.

They told him not to be afraid, that everything was going to be all right. He drifted in and out of consciousness. At times he believed he was no longer in his hospital room. He believed he was in some kind of strange operating room, with large white panels on the walls.

The next morning, he was woken up by the room nurse. He felt quiet a bit better and asked for breakfast.

Everyone was amazed. They didn't expect him to recover without a transplant. They did further tests on him and it turned out he no longer showed signs of liver damage and would not need a transplant after all.

To this day, though the man still carries the hepatitis virus in his blood, he has not shown any signs of liver damage, nor has he had a re-occurence of the disease.

Conclusion

The world of contact phenomena is exceedingly complex and cannot accurately be scrutinized solely by human standards. By it's very nature, encounters with alien beings will have an element that is alien to human understanding. This is why, when looking at any individual alien contact event, one has to keep in mind that by human standards it could seem to make little or no sense. When you consider many events all at once, the pattern of alien thinking becomes a bit clearer.

Of all the underlying themes we have seen in the accounts in this book, one theme stands clear. Despite what we, as humans, think of the alien methodology, it is clear the aliens believe that what they are doing is benefiting humankind. No longer can any educated and informed interested party ignore the reports of hundreds, perhaps thousands of individuals that indicate medical experiments are not the objective of alien visitors. There is simply too much evidence to indicate that there is much more going on.

When considering any reports of contact with alien intelligence, one must keep in mind just that; they are not only intelligent, but they are alien. Surely, if they are smart enough to build ships to get them here in the first place, and they can do all they have demonstrated — such as adjusting matter so it can pass through walls — they can do simple things like draw logical conclusions without testing an entire population.

Could everything aside from those events of a medical nature be alien created illusion? This is not likely when you consider the emotional and psychological effects

216

these encounters have on the people experiencing them. These are tangible events that affect their lives.

If the community created by the aliens were merely an illusion to pacify their human guinea pigs, how could these people find each other here on Earth and recall events to each other that both remember with such clarity and detail? It is far more than mere illusion that these people are coming together across the face of the Earth and re-establishing the relationships they have in the alien community. It is far more. It is literally Earth changing.

As people find each other, and share their common memories, the fear of ridicule and lack of self-confidence in the truth of their experiences is lost, to be replaced with a sure sense of their own validity and a confidence of what the truth is. This empowers them and they become better able to cope with their contacts. Soon, more of their memories of life in the alien environment begin to return.

Once they, as individuals, and we, as a people, accept this expanded view of the abduction experience, we are forced to look beyond the standard template of emotionally barren aliens collecting and raping humans for the purpose of creating some super alien-human hybrid race that will someday replace human beings on planet Earth. In this new view, we must consider accounts that suggest not only do the aliens have feelings and emotions, but those feelings and emotions are often expressed — in such forms as compassion — for humans. In this new view, we must consider that the aliens are not only here for their own purposes, but also to aid humankind through a time of turmoil.

Have we then returned full circle to the time of the galactic brotherhood touted in the 1950's? That is doubtful. Though some abductees still talk about galactic federations of planets, and claim that the aliens are here to help usher the human race into such a federation, evidence does not support this. If assimilating the planet into some greater galactic government was the point of contact, it would only make sense that far more than a scant two to five percent of the population would have to be involved in the decision.

Other theories for alien intervention suggest that the Earth just happens to be in the center of some kind of intergalactic battle, and that good and bad aliens are constantly flying around the Earth, making war, signing treaties, breaking treaties and bartering to be the masters of mankind. Accounts suggest that though there seems to be more than one alien race here on Earth, and though they may not always agree, this theory of a great intergalactic war is greatly over exaggerated.

One aspect of abductions we did not examine in this book, but bears mentioning, is that of apparent out-of-the-body abductions. In OBE abductions, subjects report they are taken out of their bodies and brought someplace else. These types of events are far harder to verify because they seem to be extremely individualized, thus we did not receive more than one or two that were like any others. This lack of consistency excluded them from our research, but means nothing in respect to their validity.

Abductees are told, time and time again, that the purpose of contact is that both Earth and the aliens' world are facing some great catastrophic disasters. The aliens have found that by helping the Earth overcome or survive these disasters, they will ultimately help their own people with their own problem. The nature and complexity of these disasters varies from account to account, but the concept of the alien's helping us as they help themselves is constant.

As you have seen in the one hundred accounts in this book, many things that the aliens do fit into the above theory far better than they fit into the theories of mad scientists, or galactic freedom fighters.

It must be pointed out, one more time, that the events in this book are not unique in any way. They are actually relatively common. Many abductees remember such things but are reluctant to speak about them because they do not fit into the standard template of what an abduction is supposed to entail. Because these types of events are seldom, if ever, re-enacted on television, abductees who remember experiencing such things often wonder if they are wrong to remember them.

The question of energy also needs to be addressed. What exactly is the energy the aliens talk about, and try to test and promote in their subjects? Accounts indicate that it could be some kind of mind/soul energy, or what might more commonly be called, psychic energy. It has often been noted that most — if not all — abductees believe themselves to be more psychic than the average person. There is much to support this assumption. Are the abductees chosen because of their inherent psychic skills or are these skills a by-product of the abduction experience?

Either way, many abductees believe they are not only trained to develop and use psychic skills, but they are a necessary part of the job they face after the time of changes foretold to them by the aliens.

These skills also appear to be the glue that connects abductees together. It appears as if there is some kind of psychic connection between all abductees. Once abductees are aware of others, they report they can easily feel when the other is sad, happy, hurt or sick. They tend to know what the other is thinking and they are sure the other knows their thoughts as well. This effect is far stronger if the two contactees already had an established relationship in the alien environment.

Why would the aliens develop these energies in people? Could it be that these contactees already hold a powerful tool that the aliens are trying to help them control and nurture? Perhaps the aliens want to be sure that people with these powerful tools will use them to assist the aliens in their own time of peril. They assure this cooperation by early intervention in the lives of these people.

You may question the strength of this energy as a tool. If accounts are correct, those in control of human affairs on planet Earth have no doubt of the importance of these tools. If accounts are accurate, one has to wonder if those human organizations that initiated the kidnappings reported in this book succeeded in recruiting anyone. If so, one also needs to question what those recruits were trained to do.

It should also be pointed out that of all the accounts we received, and all the people we spoke to, the accounts involving kidnapping by humans appeared to create more trauma in the victim than any of the accounts of abduction by the aliens' reported by the same subjects.

So, what have we learned by looking at one hundred accounts of abduction and contact? We believe we have learned, and demonstrated at least the following things:

1. Aliens do not think like humans. To look at their actions in a human perspective makes it difficult to see their motives.

2. Humans do not think like aliens. These visitors appear to suffer from the same problem we do. They tend to look at human actions from their alien perspective, thus sometimes missing the human point.

3. There is more to alien abduction than sperm and ovum collection. There is much more.

4. A time of great change is coming for planet Earth. Abductees are being prepared to not only survive this change, but rebuild after it.

5. Events suggest that there is also a great catastrophe befalling the alien planet and they will need assistance from Earth to overcome it.

6. The skills needed to overcome these disasters must be practiced and mastered.

7. The aliens have developed and maintained a community of experiencers in their environment.

8. These communities include bases and cities where humans meet and interact.

9. Members of these communities are coming together to recreate their communities here on Earth. As they do, the structure of our society is changing on a global scale.

Though some readers may not agree with some or all of the above statements, one thing can be agreed on. The truth of alien encounters is becoming harder and harder to deny. The reality of visitors to planet Earth interacting with humans is becoming more clear each day. The realization that there is more going on than meets the eye is Earth-changing in itself. That alone makes it probably the most important social movement in the history of the world.

The Alien Abduction Survival Guide
by Michelle LaVigne- Wedel

This book is a practical look at problems faced by abduction experiencers. Fore each problem it presents a solution that has been tested and really works! Thousands agree, it is a must have for contactees, support groups and researchers, as well as anyone else interested in the world of alien contact.

Updated for the new millennium with chapters on how to get help on the Internet and how to cope with alien social restructuring!

Also contains:
Foreword by Marc Davenport [author Visitors From Time]
Introduction by Paul Wedel [author Prophecy's Edge]
Commentary by Betty Andreasson Luca [well known abductee]

Comments from readers:

"I heartily recommend reading this book" — Betty Andreasson Luca

"Now I know I'm not going crazy. ...Thank you for writing this book" — Cheryl, abductee in TX

The Alien Abduction Survival Guide

Millennium Edition

Michelle LaVigne - Wedel
Foreword by Marc Davenport
Introduction by Paul Wedel

Winner of the Albright award for Best UFO book in 1995

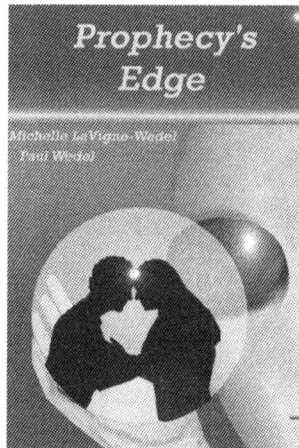

Lessons
by Michelle LaVigne- Wedel
with, Alex

By now you know about ET schools where humans are enrolled
and taught. But what exactly is taught in these UFO high
schools?

It is time to find out. Lessons is exactly that; Lessons from the
ET school, presented in the exact form they are during
abduction events.
The lessons cover such things as:
The basic principals of reality
The Nature of the Universe
and What all the genetic material is being used for
Plus much, much more.

Caution: This book
could possibly
change the way you
look at yourself,
your life, your
world and the
universe!

Prepare to
be
astonished!

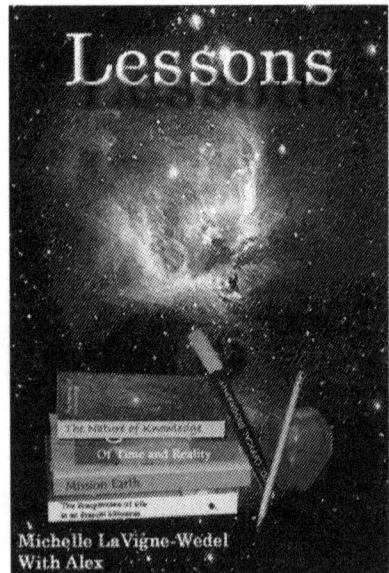

Lessons

The Nature of Knowledge
Of Time and Reality
Mission Earth

Michelle LaVigne-Wedel
With Alex

For more information on Sweetgrass Press Titles and Authors
Check our our website at:
http://www.sweetgrasspress.com

Email: info@sweetgrasspress.com

Sweetgrass Press also recommends the following websites:

Voices of the Earth
http://www.earthvoices.org

For more information on Paul and Michelle Wedel visit

http://www.sweetgrasspress/wedelbio.html

You can write to Paul and Michelle:

Michelle LaVigne Wedel & Paul Wedel
C/O Sweetgrass Press
P.O. Box 1862
Merrimack, NH 03054

Email to:

paulwedel@sweetgrasspress.com
mwedel@sweetgrasspress.com

www.ingramcontent.com/pod-product-compliance
Lightning Source LLC
Chambersburg PA
CBHW022015090426

42739CB00006BA/148